MORE HOME

Alice Thomas Ellis was born in Liverpool and educated at Bangor Grammar School and Liverpool School of Art. She is the author of five widely praised novels, *The Sin Eater*, *The Birds of the Air*, *The 27th Kingdom*, *The Other Side of the Fire* and *Unexplained Laughter*. Her most recent book, *Secrets of Strangers*, is a study of juvenile delinquency written with a psychiatrist, Tom Pitt-Aiken. Since 1985 she has written a weekly column in the *Spectator* under the title 'Home Life', which has gained her a readership even wider than her novels. She lives in London and Wales with her husband and five children.

The entire family is still
loth to contradict Janet...

ALICE THOMAS ELLIS

More
Home Life

with illustrations by Zé

FLAMINGO
Published by Fontana Paperbacks

First published by Gerald Duckworth & Co. Ltd 1987

This Flamingo edition first published
in 1988 by Fontana Paperbacks
8 Grafton Street, London W1X 3LA

Flamingo is an imprint of Fontana Paperbacks,
a division of the Collins Publishing Group

Copyright © Alice Thomas Ellis 1987

Printed and bound in Great Britain by
William Collins Sons & Co. Ltd, Glasgow

For Janet

CONTENTS

Liberated lady

Well, after all that fuss it wasn't such a bad Christmas after all – really quite agreeable. I always feel a bit daunted as I regard 15 shining expectant faces and glance from them to the turkey crouching in a threatening stance, waiting to be carved, but as I've gone quite limp by that time anyway I leave the carving to any delightful gentleman who cares to try his skill: Michael this year, and a very good job he made of it – *and* the ham. Someone presided over the claret with his usual urbanity, and I even remembered to put the gravy on the table. We all looked particularly lovely, especially me in a glitzy coat that Beryl gave me, which made me rather resemble a salmon who had been muscle-pumping, since it has *Dynasty*-type shoulder pads.

At the moment I am wearing fleecy cotton trousers, a hooded anorak, a full-lenth coat-dress, a cardie made by Janet from the wool of Icelandic sheep and a fingerless mitten (which I nicked from Jemma) on my writing hand which has gone numb. I look like a cross between Old Mother Riley, a Knight Templar and a troll, and people can scarce forbear to smile as their eyes light on me. I don't care. It was so cold when we arrived in Wales that the lock had frozen on the fuel store and there are Jack Frost patterns on the windows. It got a touch warmer when the snow came but no one is inclined to remove his hat and coat, even with the Aga and all the fires blazing.

The countryside looks more beautiful than at any other

time of year; pared to the bone and bright with dead bracken, green pale with rimed grass. A full moon rose over the mountain as we were getting out of the car and I wondered why anyone ever stays in London – until I remembered the 'summer' and the relentless rain which gave the whole country the air of a miserable slut. The clarity of the light now makes everything cheerful even with all growth in abeyance. Still, I'm dashed glad I'm not a peasant living here 500 years ago. It must have been remarkably uncomfortable having to rely on smoky fires and the warmth of the animals shacked up beyond the wooden partition. I don't know how they managed without immersion heaters and the odd electric radiator as back up. I wonder how they forced themselves to wash or whether they ever did. Even now there is not the usual run on the bathroom facilities (except for the daughter who takes a shower about three times a day, causing the water to get low).

Speaking of the daughter, she inconvenienced herself a few days before Christmas. She demanded that as we were too busy to go ourselves we should send a taxi to fetch her a selection of sugar and cholesterol from the hamburger joint, and when I demurred she, being a spirited child, shot into the study and slammed the door with such aplomb and conviction that it utterly refused to open again. After a while, foreseeing that she was likely to spend Christmas walled up in the west wing she began to wail in a plaintive fashion, but we were all, by this time, suffering from the giggles and too weak to apply the jemmy to the lock, even had we possessed one. God is not mocked, I told her through the intransigent door when I regained my composure. In the end, showing the determination and ingenuity which characterize her (apart from the fiendish temper) she dropped the library steps out of the back window and clambered down into the garden of her friend Isobel, turning up at the front of the house wearing a jaunty expression. I was too reduced by now to remonstrate with her, and she began to complain

12

that she had left her blue nail varnish and her blackhead-removing cream behind. 'Tough,' said Janet, who takes a firmer line than me. Having reared only one daughter I cannot count myself an expert on the subject, but even with the experience of five sons I'm not sure that girls are not more trouble. Better company for a mother in many ways but more trouble in many more.

I wonder about other peoples' daughters since last night, when four little girls came with the carol singers, opened their tiny mouths and emitted, with entire confidence, the most lovely sounds – new Welsh carols, most of them, most of which I understood one word in 25, but sounding perfectly enchanting. They seemed to me as good as gold and I do so hope that sometimes they slam doors.

The daughter is now out on the hills sledging on a bin bag, with pellets whistling about her head as the guns take their toll of the pheasants, and in a while, as darkness descends, I expect I shall have to put on the wellies and go and look for her. I don't know how it happened, but I have a feeling she's the result of women's lib.

The right approach

Sometimes Beryl laughs so much she has to lie down. She did the other day. We were in our local trying to have a talk without disturbance – something impossible in the home – and a foreign gentleman apparently mistook me for a lady of the night. I can't imagine why. I was wearing my ladylike grey flannel and had my hair scraped right back. Nonetheless he kept telling me that he had just 15 minutes and more or less insisting that I nip outside and help him to occupy them.

I told him I was a married lady and very religious and he got quite indignant. He would tap himself on the chest saying he had all the love, and then he'd attempt to do the same thing to me, saying I had the experience. Sauce. It was at that point that Beryl had to lie down, sobbing with uncontrollable hysteria. I was trying to maintain a serious demeanour because I didn't particularly want to hurt the wretched man's feelings, and also these scenes can get quite tense if one is not careful. Fortunately the 15 minutes elapsed and he was required back at his place of work.

We took Jeff to Mass last Sunday, creeping into the pub beforehand for a fortifying vodka. What was my astonishment – for this is far from Jeff's manor – to hear a voice saying 'Hi, Jeff.' 'Hallo Boris,' responded Jeffrey with what seemed to me to be modified enthusiasm. Boris bought us all a drink and insisted on lending Jeff a fiver, so I said, as we departed, 'What a nice man', and Jeffrey agreed that he was charming but added that he had a nasty job.

'Oh poor thing,' we said sympathetically, 'what does he do?'

'He's a burglar,' said Jeff.

That's one of the things I like about this part of the world – you meet all sorts. Only last week I was trotting towards the station averting eyes from the winos who stand or sit by the back wall of the cinema, a line of pee leading from each to the gutter, reminding one of the chickens and chalk lines, when a young man darted out a doorway requesting the loan of a match. No point here in pretending not to have seen him, so we got into conversation. He had two companions – one utterly silent, and one a pretty girl. He said they were Irish travelling people and I didn't like to ask what that meant – gypsies, tinkers, or just Irish people who got about a lot? With the novelist's interest in raw material I enquired their names. He said reassuringly that he was known as Jerry the Street Fighter. So I hastily asked the name of the girl.

'Mary de Rothschild,' she responded.

'Pardon?' I said.

'Mary the Lost Child,' she repeated. That made me want to cry, so I departed the poorer by a match and a couple of quid. Jerry offered me a swig from his bottle and I said I was a teetotaller. He intimated that it might be nice if they all came home with me, and then he kissed me. I really must change my perfume. When I *think* of the strictures I put upon the daughter about not talking to strangers.

A couple of years ago I broke Rule Number One. I had been to see Caroline and instead of calling a cab to the house I went off to pick one up at Brompton Road. Unfortunately the pubs were just emptying and every time I hailed a taxi it was whipped away by pairs of very alarming men, some bold in black leather hung about with chains, and some with Mexican-type moustaches. I was not disposed to argue with them so I stood in the rain growing quietly desperate. After a while a private car drew up and a gentleman leaned out and asked if he could give me a lift. Before you could say 'rape' I had hopped in. Can you believe it? I realized immediately, of course, that I was a much more foolish person than I had previously supposed and began a very Cheltenham tea-table conversation about the weather and the cost of private education in my most modulated tones. He was a dear kind man up from the country for the day and he drove me straight home – some considerable distance – declining to come in and meet my husband and join us in a cup of coffee. I don't know what he must have thought. *No* well brought up woman gets into the cars of strange men. I was lucky there, but I have instructed my friends never to let me out alone after a convivial evening. I can't be trusted.

The nuns used to observe a ploy known as 'custody of the eyes' which sounds rather disgustingly culinary and reminds me of St Lucy. They don't do it any more since Vatican II, beaming out frankly at the world and exchanging greetings on the street, but I'm going to do it in future. I shall keep the gaze fixed on the middle distance, glancing neither to right nor left. I'll probably break my neck.

The wrong place

I had difficulty brushing my teeth the other morning because the bathroom basin was occupied by a cat, the pet of my friend the analyst. This large white Persian has a penchant for dripping taps and is also frequently found in the kitchen sink. He is a most amiable and beautiful beast, name of Focus, but it is disconcerting to find a cat in the basin. Can you imagine spitting round a cat?

Animals in the wrong place are always disconcerting. There is something hibernating in the rafters above my bed. I hear it stirring irritably in its sleep and suspect it of being a squirrel, since there is often a sound as of nuts being rolled around. Squirrels, in my view, should confine themselves to trees, just as horses should limit their horizons to fields. Many years ago Alfie was alone in the country with a selection of children. He was determined to do everything absolutely correctly and one day as he was busily being me – that is, he had the cottage door open, his coat on, a fag in his face and a glass of bitter to hand as he peeled the carrots for *soupe bonne femme* – when the kitchen suddenly darkened. A storm is coming up, thought Alfie vaguely, continuing with the good work. Then he chanced to glance at the window and observed a blue and cloudless sky. Turning, he discovered that George, the horse who was employed to haul logs out of the forest, had got himself wedged in the cottage door. The next part of the story is unclear. It seems that the children had to scuttle between George's legs to get in and out of the cottage, making helpful suggestions such as tying a rope around that part of George which it would be coarse to mention and dragging him out backwards. I don't know how the situation resolved itself but the door was horseless when I arrived, though Alfie looked a bit frail and was inordinately pleased to see me.

My friend Virginia had a worse horse experience. She once owned a farm in Italy and one day, lying blamelessly in her bath, she was joined by a horse. It was like that TV ad for bath-salts only less romantic. It had walked up the stairs but couldn't get down again. She had to sidle round it, dripping, and send for some neighbouring farmers to come with block and tackle.

Then there was the time Beryl was staying with us and our blasted bulldog chased two heifers into the conifer plantation – quite the wrong place for cows, since the firs are planted scarcely inches apart. They hurdled the fence like fillies and took to the forest at the speed of light, the bulldog in hot pursuit. There followed a *mauvais quart d'heure* with me attempting to murder the dog at the same time as rounding up the cows. I slid down the forest slopes on my bottom, doing no good at all to a rather decent coat and skirt. Beryl laughed so much she had to lie down again – on the path, still clutching her plate of lunch: sausages and beans, I remember.

I must go and get Cadders out of his favourite wrong place now and put him out in the snow. His nose is a bit put out of joint by the presence of Focus and he spends *all* his time on the sleeping-bags in the airing cupboard. Focus is doubtless in the kitchen sink, and if not he will be contentedly kipping on somebody's bed. Probably mine. Quite the wrong place.

Snowed under

It is getting very deep and crisp out there – and uneven,
since the old snow has thawed where we have walked on it
and then frozen again and new snow is masking the dangers.
Very fine stuff is falling in a carelessly determined fashion,
and I believe we may be snowed in. I have alerted the family
in London to the fact that we may be some time. My last
visitors narrowly made it to the main road after an interesting
drive along the lane, where they were baulked by a frozen
hill and had to slither in circles until they reached the
alternative lane. They took all the ash from the fires in plastic
bags to spread before their wheels, which was quite con-
venient for me since I didn't have to push it to the ashpit in
the wheelbarrow. Our last load of garbage, which we left
neatly bagged by the gate ready for the Cyngor Dosbarth,
had been unbagged by wild beasts and presented a most
unlovely appeareance until the snow covered it. I was going
to rebag it: only now I can't, because it's all frozen to the
ground and the neighbouring bushes. Good.

The maintenance of neatness and personal hygiene is
problematic in these conditions. People display a reluctance
to remove their clothes or immerse themselves in the bath,
which is at best lukewarm and threatens after a while to form
a thin sheet of ice, imprisoning one beneath it. At least, that
is the feeling. The daughter and her friend Philippa are
exceptional in this. They keep running off to the barn in their
bare feet and dressing-gowns to wash their hair. The daughter in particular regards wellies as inelegant and persists in
walking through the snow in pointed, fashionable shoes with

silly little heels. I tell her if she doesn't freeze to death she will undoubtedly develop bunions, but she doesn't care. But then she is made of sterner stuff than me. She spent the whole summer (which wasn't all that much warmer than now) swimming in the mountain pools and drying off in a force eight gale. Cadders conspicuously lacks the Captain Oates spirit. I show him the door. He looks at the prevailing circumstances with a 'Sod that for a game of soldiers' expression and scuttles under the stairs while I pursue him with a broom.

Still, I can't complain, because being snowed in in the country is my dream, offering the perfect opportunity to write a long introspective novel with no distractions. It gets less dreamy when the electricity fails, but I have hundreds of candles and the little girls trudge back and forth to the log pile, so we have roaring fires. It's wonderful how much time you can waste messing about with a log fire, poking it here, poking it there. The washing is quite good too. 'It has to be done,' I say, virtuously crouching by the washing-machine filling it with bed sheets, while a pile of blank white paper sits reproachfully on my desk. Then there are always crumbs to be swept up, and the children have to be fed. I really enjoy cooking mince and dumplings when the alternative is getting down to the deathless prose. I have yet to meet a writer who wouldn't rather peel a banana than apply himself to the pen. I believe if I were locked in a windowless room with a deadline I would spend the time trying to tunnel out rather than get on with it.

Oh, well, here we go again. It is two days later and we are no longer snowed in. This time we're flooded in. The snow all melted overnight and our flanking streams – normally mild little chaps of the bowler hat, briefcase and umbrella type – have gone berserk, busting through the banks and roaring in a thoroughly macho fashion. I stood for hours watching waves breaking round the boles of the trees to pour

'The daughter... persists in walking through the snow in pointed, fashionable shoes...'

into the meadow. Two sheep are marooned on a slight eminence. Yesterday Janet had to be transported from the village through banks of snow by the kindly gamekeeper in his Land-Rover. Today we should have to have recourse to the water bailiff and a canoe. Janet says we should have saved all the corks which have passed through this house and constructed ourselves a raft. She wonders wistfully whether if we flung a whisky bottle on to the tide with an imploring note in it someone would return it, primed. I think it unlikely. Anyway there is absolutely no shortage of water to drink. I have just warned the daughter that she would appear very foolish if her epitaph read 'Drowned in a Meadow'.

Back to the fray

I can't really claim that the Christmas hols in the country were uneventful, what with frost, tempest and flood – Janet had to go to the village by tractor at one point because the lane had turned into a stream. She said she felt a proper lemon in her fur coat and moon-boots with the two little girls standing in the pig nuggets with a huge feathered wash spraying out high behind them. I missed this pretty sight, and I'm rather annoyed, since Janet's maiden name indicates that she is descended from Queen Boudicca (as I believe she is now spelt) of the Iceni and the scene must have been somewhat evocative of that lady steaming along in her chariot. I feel cheated of a good laugh.

Still, even with all that weather going on, the country is more peaceful than London. Apart from the immediate family and the hired help, the only contact with the human race consists of glimpses of a distant shepherd, or Sir chasing his pheasants. If I ever feel lonely I can telephone Someone, although the phone is situated in a particularly chilly bit of the house and one's hands tend to get frozen to the receiver. It is all very quiet and makes one feel that one's desiccated old spirit has been briefly put in water. Now London does not give one that impression. Living in London is rather like living in the middle of the motorway and I have the sensation that my feet haven't touched the ground since I returned. After days of placidly plodding about carrying Aga fuel and logs and doing simple rustic tasks, I found myself involved in two luncheon parties, four dinner parties, two photographic sessions and a trip to the Arts Council. I know people who can cope with all that, I can't, and drink doesn't help. It's very nice while you're drinking it but you regret it the following day, particularly if that day holds a photographic session and the bags under your eyes are making your jaw line sag.

One of these sessions was particularly interesting. A nice young fellow called Nic came along to take a few simple snapshots with a mass of equipment which would not have been inadequate on the set of a biblical epic, and he chose a room and put up all his stands and sheets and umbrellas and spread cables all over the place, and then he plugged in a sort of arc light and everything fused. The third son – rather brilliantly in my estimation, since these matters are a closed book to me – mended the fuse, and Nic plugged in his light again, whereupon everything fused again. By the time it was sorted out we were all faintly hysterical and had less difficulty than usual in pasting grins on our faces. I never could understand how people are expected to smile while under-going an experience as horrible as being photographed. Even Jemma, who is an actress and should be used to it, remem-bered an important engagement some distance away and fled like a rabbit at the suggestion that she should be included.

After the fuses were mended, the drain flooded: a much nastier flood than the one in Wales, which was only melted snow, since it consisted of the effluent from the washing machine and cannot be doing any good at all to the castor-oil plant, about whose roots it ebbs and flows. The trouble is that plumbers are out all day engaged on unblocking other people's drains and I can never remember to ring them in the evening. The same thing goes for electricians and other artisans. They used to have homebound wives to take frantic messages; but now, I think, they're all divorced, or their wives go out to work. We were very lucky to find a new window-cleaner, because the last one dematerialized. Alfie's brother Peter has taken up this avocation, and the other day

Someone aderat forte

when we came home from doing the shopping there was Peter busily polishing windows and in the kitchen towering over the Aga was his bull mastiff, Portia. She was very friendly, but the cats spent the morning in an alcove beside St Martin and we were very nice to her.

Someone is the opposite of me and detests the country, much preferring London. I really knew I was home again when I heard him talking to himself while shaving. Perhaps there are lots of people who talk to themselves while shaving. How would I know? But I bet there are remarkably few who do it in Ancient Greek.

Ghost stories

It is, as somebody has remarked, a small world. I had arranged with my friend the analyst that I would go and stay in the flat of his brother, which is situated in Aylesbury, in order to do an awful lot of work without distraction since I knew absolutely nobody there. Then my favourite cousin, Mahalia, who now lives in Pennsylvania and whom I haven't seen since we used to rip our knickers sliding down the gravel in the quarry, rang up to say she was here on a visit and was staying with her youngest brother in Aylesbury. The minute I saw her I felt we should not sit down and sip sherry but dash out and climb trees. An enterprising and fun-loving cousin is perhaps the best sort of relation one can have. Her brother, whom I never really knew because the last time I saw him he was in nappies and I didn't like babies much, has also turned out to be the sort of relation one can appreciate, which is sadly rare. He does wonderfully intricate carving and sees ghosts.

Actually my cousin does more than just see them. He fights them. Their family house in Canning Street, Liverpool, is comprehensively haunted. One night my cousin who had gone up to bed with a bottle of milk (*milk*, mark you) was lying down with his hands behind his head when his wrists were gripped by an unseen assailant. He was much too astonished and frightened to wonder who had grabbed him, but fought back vigorously. Alerted by the clamour, my aunt and two of her daughters rushed up to find out wha' was going on, but the door had locked itself. Still struggling, he contrived to open it, and when things calmed down they discovered that the floor was awash with milk and blood. The bottle had been knocked over and my cousin had cut a tendon in his foot on the broken glass. There was absolutely no sign of another human being. That story gives me gooseflesh, so I would know it was authentic even if my cousin did not display the veracity which typifies my father's side of the family.

My aunt used to be visited by a phantom in evening dress who would lean against her bedroom door eyeing her thoughtfully, and one day a friend called Jimmy who happened to be a half-caste – this is only relevant because my cousin says he definitely went pale – met a wraith on the landing who gibbered at him. At the time he assumed it was a family member fooling about and marched into the sitting-room demanding that the idiot own up, but there was nobody missing and nobody had stirred. This always happens with real ghosts – if I may use that phrase. People assume that the visitant is corporeal until they realize that that is impossible and only then are they frightened – except for my cousin, of course, who was scared out of his wits by what he supposed to be a burglarious assassin. He says that since my aunt died the house is dying too. He had to go there to see his sisters and drove down the motorway at about 25 miles an hour filled with horrid forebodings. The paint is peeling off the family portraits, the paper is coming off the walls and he says that all the evil entities which had been kept at bay by the presence of my aunt, a good and extraordinary woman (she could mend shoes, among other things), were now closing in and taking over. But then the same thing is happening to the whole of Liverpool. I stand with Jung, who thought it was the centre of the world. I loved that city and its people with a passion and now I can't bear to go there. As Beryl (who feels the same way as me and Jung) says: 'Somebody has murdered Liverpool and got away with it.'

I forgot to tell you about one occult experience which I share with my cousin. We both, when little, floated downstairs. My cousin told his mother immediately and she, without looking up from her ironing, said, 'Of course you did.' I didn't tell anybody, but I must have been 19 before it occurred to me as odd, and I wondered if I really had. I still wonder in my sillier moments, because I *know* I did. If anyone has a rational explanation for this phenomenon he will kindly keep it to himself.

Every modern inconvenience

I always thought I didn't like the Modern much, and I was right, I don't like reinforced concrete, or formica, or Andy Warhol, and I hate square coffee cups and abstract murals, and I utterly loathe shopping precincts with pattered pavements and plenty of space for people to strew their chicken 'n' chips packets and polystyrene mugs. I got lost in one the other day. Everyone had said comfortingly that no one could get lost in Aylesbury, it was impossible. But I can. I can get lost in Trafalgar Square with no trouble at all, and when everything is modern I get hopelessly confused. How, I ask myself, does anyone ever remember which tower block he lives in, and does it matter? I had tracked down Marks & Spencer's, which I favour because I trust their milk and their arsenic-free chickens, and it also makes me vaguely think of the Church, since wherever you go there it is, completely familiar and offering the same services. I would much rather have a corner shop with a white-coated grocer climbing on stools to reach the nutmeg, but now that they've all been driven away I have reluctantly come to terms with M & S. I can usually find the things I want despite their policy of keeping the customers on their toes by moving the wares more frequently than seems necessary – 'Where are you hiding the eggs this week?' one demands fretfully.

So I bagged a few essentials and made for home, feeling quite pleased with myself, when I realized I had lost my sense of direction and was also carrying rather a lot of clanking shopping. I determined that I absolutely would not weaken and hail a taxi, and by dint of asking every other passer-by I finally arrived back where I had started from: a modern flat. Now, to be fair, it is an extremely nice modern flat with every convenience and no draughts, but we couldn't make the hot water work because the means by which the water gets hot is highly technological and sophisticated and quite beyond the man in the street. I don't like lying on the floor in the ashes, blowing a reluctant flame in the boiler, but I can do it. What I can't do is figure out wildly complicated systems of switches and wiring that require a person with a degree in such matters – so the water stayed cold.

I didn't mind all that much, since I didn't stay too long, but it must be awkward for people who live with these wonders of modern science and are as idiotic as myself. I often think how pleasantly simple it would be to live in a tent and never have to send for the man to mend the dish-washer. For one thing he is always so cross – not only at being called out, but because he so disapproves of people who mishandle dish-washers. No RSPCA inspector faced with a battered pet could be more irate than the man who mends the dish-washer as he glares into its maw and realizes that we have somehow buggered it up. I don't like washing dishes by hand either, but apart from blocking it with potato peelings there isn't a great deal you can do to damage the kitchen sink. I would rather make toast on a fork before the fire than entrust it to a mad electric toaster which might burn it, or suddenly fling it ceilingwards, or merely refuse to relinquish it, and I can't bear ovens which turn themselves on and off. The near right-hand burner on the oven in this flat, which was the one I preferred, was also the one which wouldn't respond to the automatic switch, and there wasn't a thing I could do about it. I would almost rather rub two twigs together or wait for a flash of lightning to ignite the kindling beneath the cooking pot. You would know where you were.

But I must not give way to ingratitude. It was very comfortable and warm and I did a lot of work, and the retired gentleman's gentleman who lives downstairs showed me where to secrete the garbage. His flat was identical to the one I was in, which gave me a peculiar feeling. I felt like an Old Person, or a pussy in a cattery, or possibly a privileged nun or a highly indulged prisoner, something faintly institutional anyway. Even the flat's proud owner demonstrated compassion as he left me all on my own – doing porridge, as he put it. I think that even when I am very aged I will live in a house even more aged than myself with inconveniences that I can handle.

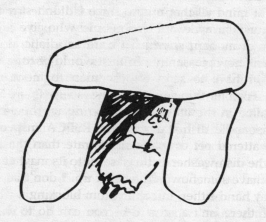

'A house more venerable than myself'

Unready money

I like money. That is, it is my preferred means of completing pecuniary transactions. I'm not particularly keen on handing over wads of currency of the realm, but at least one knows where one is, whereas the chequebook is a snare and a delusion, containing misleading numbers of blank cheques when none of the money that the bank contains is rightfully one's own.

Sometimes of course this works in one's favour. The bailiff popped in again the other day on one of his usual visits and sat sipping a glass of Soave, speculating on the value of the dining-room table and a few battered knick-knacks, while Janet hastily rang the bank to ascertain the situation round there. The current account and the bailiff's demand did not precisely synchronize, but I insouciantly signed a cheque and sent him away happy, which I could not have done had I had to rely on the contents of the sock under the mattress. Anyway, I think banks owe their customers a lot by way of compensation for the aggravation they cause them. My friend Zélide came in the other day quivering with rage after the cash dispenser had first agreed and then wilfully refused to give her any money. It spat a bit of paper at her, asking how much she wanted, and then said she couldn't have it. Questioned, the man in the bank said she had probably proffered her card too forcefully. If machines take offence at the slightest thing, what is to become of us all? She went to another cash dispenser, which insolently told her to go to Hampstead.

Some supermarkets now permit people to pay for their

purchases with a horrid little card which has to be inserted into a little machine and takes ages. I get very restive when I find myself stuck behind a person who has been stocking up for his bunker and has abandoned the habit of carrying money in favour of this pestilential card. I wile away the time staring at the extraordinary things he has bought and wondering what his lifestyle can possibly be. Some people buy 14 packets of biscuits at a time. Are they giving a kiddies' party, or do they just constantly like to nibble? The other day the man behind me had one arm and three bags of oranges and a packet of carrots in his basket. I found myself wondering wildly not about the dish he planned to prepare but the simple mechanical problem of getting all the peel off. This made me feel heartless and even crosser at the delay which offers idle minds time for such fancies.

The account card is a rich source of embarrassment and annoyance. Many's the time that Janet and I have whistled carelessly, fingering lengths of cloth and gazing into the distance while a suspicious assistant rings all round the store to see if our credit is good. I believe it is the case that banks are bound to honour cheques written on anything, not just the neat little pages in the book. You could, apparently, drive a cow into a bank with 'Pay cash' inscribed on its flanks and they would have to cough up. Sometimes, twentieth in the queue, watching the staff ambling about discussing the meaning of life while one teller sits at one of those many little windows, I would gladly drive a herd of heifers all over the establishment. In the paper today I read that soon even the chequebook will be redundant and we shall all have to master some electronic device in order to lay our hands on our lucre. I somehow know instinctively that this is not going to work to our advantage. It is not going to save us time and anxiety. It is going to be another reason for the bank to make its maddening little charges and enable the staff to get off to the golf-course while the light lasts.

If money is, as it were, going out of fashion, then rather than rely on all that abstruse technology I would prefer to go back to a system of barter. Haggling at the till over the relative value of the week's shopping and the fur coat your aunt left you would certainly not save much time, but it would be much more fun.

March

Generation gap

The daughter (12) has just had her rubella injection and has had to sign a form declaring that she realizes she mustn't get pregnant in the next three months. Janet said she must at all costs avoid gooseberry bushes and if a stork should fly past she must avert her eyes. Then I asked sympathetically if the injection had hurt, and Janet said, 'Just a little prick,' and the daughter shrieked with laughter.

I didn't even know the facts of life until I was 12, and when I was told I didn't believe them. I was 19 before Fritz Spiegl told me about lesbians and (quite the little Queen Victoria) I didn't believe that either. I remember the occasion vividly. I was walking along Princes Boulevard in Liverpool with Fritz, and he mentioned this funny lady. When it became clear that I didn't know what he was talking about he very kindly explained. It was most interesting. I *do* owe a lot to Fritz. He used to play me records of the music of Mozart and Scarlatti, and after a very short while I realized that I absolutely hated it and would prefer to listen to the tap dripping. This early realization has saved me a great deal of time and trouble. I don't like pop music either and the extraordinary noises the children wear strapped to their ears. How can they bear it?

Another thing I don't understand about my children's generation is that they seem very precocious and knowing, to begin with, and then, like axolotls, they get stuck in a sort of adolescence for years and years. A friend of one of the sons got engaged recently and there were howls of anguish from all his peers bewailing the fact that he was throwing

33

'I developed a real aversion...

away his youth. As his mother pointed out reasonably, he *was* 35. I put it all down to John F. Kennedy. People were always going on as though he was a mere stripling, when he was 42. Or is it all due to the Sixties? I had a powerful impression in the Sixties that either it was just me or the rest of the world had gone barking mad. Having been an art student, I had grown out of wearing weird gear, and it was most odd to find everyone, at quite an advanced age, suddenly sprouting fuzzy hair-dos and feathers and flowers, and donning frocks with bits of mirror stuck on them. I developed a real aversion to men in medallions, and the one time I smoked hashish I felt totally dreadful. It was then, in my opinion, that the concept of childrearing took a dive, and it was just my rotton luck that I had most of my children then. It was very difficult to take a firm line with one's own when half the people one knew were permitting little Jason to throttle the cat because he felt like it and, if prevented, might grow up with a grossly distorted personality. The lunacy persists. Beryl's grandson goes to a nursery school where they refer to Jesus impartially as he/she and it is left to Beryl and her daughter to attempt to correct this impression. I expect most parents are familiar with the expression 'But teacher says . . .' No matter that teacher is all of 17 with an IQ of room-temperature and one has oneself a degree in theology and hotel management. What teacher says, goes, at least when the toddies are small. Later, of course, the toddies go through a stage of discounting what *everybody* tells them. Except for Janet. The entire family is still loth to contradict Janet.

I have been reading a book called *Good Children* by Lynette Burrows which seems to me to contain a lot of sense. I am not over-keen on books that tell you how to live, be they sex manuals or those American tomes that explain how to raise your consciousness or make the neighbours envious or Get to the Top. Manuals, it seems to me, should be about how to get the car to work. People are more complex. Still, Mrs Burrows is not dogmatic, nor full of exciting new ideas as Dr Spock tended to be, nor cruel as Truby King was – he regarded child-care as a struggle to the death for supremacy between parent and child. A crying child in his day was considered very naughty, screaming merely to put one over on its mum by seeking her attention. *Good Children* is commendably sane and down-to-earth. I disagree with the author only on the subject of television. She imagines it is difficult to prise children away from it, but this is not my experience. I have frequently found myself imploring the little ones to for goodness' sake go and watch the bloody thing and give me a spot of peace.

'My teacher says Jesus was a lady'

Building on

The other English vice is building-on. Think of the proposed extension to the National Gallery. Few Englishmen can resist the temptation to fling out a wing here, throw up a turret there. Those with more limited scope add sun lounges in the backyard, bow windows on Edwardian workers' dwellings, artistically arranged breeze blocks round the garden; or they simply replace their wooden front doors with ones of reeded glass. We have seldom been without builders since we first set up house. We added bathrooms, which was sensible, and a studio for me which turned out to be not so sensible because I find I regard it as a sort of punishment cell to which I must confine myself when work can no longer be deferred.

Ours is the end house in the Crescent and all the other houses have been leaning on it since 1840. Because of this it once threatened to fall down and had to be shored up, which necessitated the presence of builders for many months.

The only advantage of this is that they will babysit the children while you go shopping. Last year I idly remarked that it would be nice if we could go straight out of the drawing-room on to a balcony, and Someone instantly went out and ordered one.

It looks very splendid but induces delusions of grandeur and an impulse to stand smiling and waving graciously at the neighbours, while the more romantically inclined invariably go 'Romeo, Romeo, wherefore art thou . . .' as though they'd just thought of it, which is irritating.

The house in the country *had* fallen down, several hundred years ago, so builders were again essential. We were extremely fortunate in finding a local one who could handle the enormous lumps of stone which go into its construction and hoick them into place as though they were polystyrene, in marked constrast to some urban 'builders' I have known who seem entirely unfamiliar with the nature and purpose of the RSJ, the positioning of the soil pipe or the angling of the guttering. I have learned a lot about all these through bitter experience.

The pipes burst after Christmas in London, and here in Wales. The cylinder looked as though someone had left it in the fast lane on the M1 and when we turned on the mains tap the water certainly ran, but out of the walls. We had despairingly resigned ourselves to collecting buckets of water from the stream and bathing in face lotion, but when we arrived Maldwyn had mended the pipes and gone on to light the Aga – which was above and beyond the call of duty and puts him not only in the class of Master Builder but also of Best Friend.

Actually I must stop complaining, because although in London we have two sets of builders (you can see the level of addiction to which we have risen) and one lot is wearyingly hopeless, the other lot, which consists of two brothers and their school friend, is reassuringly competent. They turn up when they say they will, and come every day until the job is finished. If there is anyone in the country who finds one's pathetic gratitude for this surprising, they must be unique in never having had builders. We were fortunate also in finding some London plumbers to adjust the hot-water system. The boss was Spanish, which I found disconcerting. Oslo, Helsinki, even Amsterdam or Omsk – but a heating engineer from *Barcelona*? He was quite enchanting, his courtly foreign grace evident even through the plaster dust in which he was covered. Adjusting the hot-water system necessarily involves turning off the central heating, so I took to my bed and when a query arose as to which bit of skirting board would most conveniently accommodate an emerging pipe I came down to discuss the matter in my night-dress – a very decent and enveloping garment, I must assure you, but not really geared to withstanding the wind chill factor. After a moment, as I turned blue, he said concernedly, 'Ees there not a blanket or essomething? You are esshivering.' I have tried that in all sizes and from every angle and I cannot, I *cannot*, imagine an English plumber, no matter how motherly, saying it – not even in English.

A plumber from Bathelona

Cold comfort

If you really wanted to baffle a Texan or a Japanese or even your mother-in-law, provided she didn't hail from the East End, you could speak as follows: 'I was doing 70 down the frog when the rabbit went in the haddock.' My friend the used-car dealer made this observation the other day and I gazed at him blankly, whereupon he elaborated. He had been driving at 70 miles an hour down the frog and toad, when the rabbit hutch had failed to function in the haddock and bloater. Got it? For anyone not familiar with rhyming slang, 'road,' 'clutch' and 'motor' are the missing words. He lost me again with a reference to a jolly good cabbage he had recently attended. This turned out to be a party, springing from the phrase 'a cabbage good and hearty'. We all know about the apples and pears, but I am now becoming familiar with the more esoteric renderings, and very interesting they are. 'A run of luck' speaks for itself, but I pondered for some time before I understood that a 'kick in the orchestras' describes a form of GBH. It took me longer than it would have done normally since, I think, my brain has frozen, and this is because the weather is so confoundedly taters.*

Our plumbing problems continue to proliferate. The boiler which serves the central heating has chosen this time to spring a copious leak and surround itself with a tide which rippled in the Force 8 gale sweeping in under the door. The plumber removed the old boiler and sent off for a new one. A new one duly arrived but of the wrong type. (Everyone I

* taters in the mould = cold.

40

have told about this has said: 'But *of course* they brought the wrong boiler. This is *England*.') The man who brought it said he knew it was the wrong one but as they hadn't got the right one he thought we'd rather have the wrong one than none at all, and I can't follow his reasoning. Maybe his brain has frozen too. Another boiler has arrived and is sitting there promisingly in its cardboard box – only now the plumber is missing. I rather want to kill him but must remember to restrain myself until he has exercised his craft, when I shall, at the least, address to him a short homily. The cold is also making me spiteful. A friend was shivering and moaning the other day in the throes of incipient flu, and enquiring querulously whether we thought he'd got Aids, and I said it looked to me more like coccidiosis. I'd once seen a chicken looking the way he did and shortly afterwards it had died.

There has just been a reassuring clanking of tools heralding the arrival of the plumber and I am so relieved to see him that I am no longer cross but inclined to embrace him and offer him whisky and half my kingdom. It's the same with children. When they go off for hours leaving no clue as to their whereabouts you promise yourself that when they do reappear you will beat the living daylights out of them. But no – in they bounce and, instead of the good hiding, you make them fatted-calf butties and feebly ask them not to do it again.

The following day: I had to stop writing this because not only my brain but my right hand was frozen stiff. The plumbing situation now is quite intriguing. When the boiler was made fully operational, the plumber developed fears about the feasibility of the pump, but after some fiddling pronounced it fit. It isn't. The radiators upstairs are moderately warm but downstairs they are not. Clearly the pump does not work and the heat, as it will, is rising and is going to stay up there until some mechanical device forces it back to where it's supposed to be. There is also a new puddle sloshing round the base of the new boiler which I find very mysterious and *there is no hot water coming out of the taps*. The boiler is flaring away and sounds marvellously efficient and I can't think where the heat is going. It can't *all* be upstairs. I feel limp. Why is it we can put men on the moon but not make the hot water go round? What is it all about?

The only time this week I've felt all right was when we went to see Rosamond Lehmann who is so beautiful and enchanting that her mere presence is warming.

Now, I think, I'm going upstairs to hibernate where the heat is, or maybe I'll just have one little tumble in the sink.

Reluctant participant

I am again wondering why we go to parties where we have to stand up because most of the chairs have been removed in order to make room for us to do so. It is worse for women, because they feel it incumbent on themselves to wear smart shoes which are seldom comfortable, and I cannot see the fun in standing up with a fag in the face, a glass of (mostly despicable) hooch in one hand and something indefinable stuck on a stick in the other, bellowing pleasantries at people whom one has a needling feeling one probably knows quite well but cannot put a name to. (This inability to remember who my friends are is the reason I call absolutely everybody darling.) And – you keep asking yourself worriedly – will you ever find a taxi to take you home to bed, and what will it cost? Almost certainly your children, on learning you are going out, will have taken most of the readies to buy fish and chips. Remembering this, you torture yourself by wondering whether they have safely returned from the chippie and have had the sense to lock the door.

I sometimes describe my unwillingness to leave home as agoraphobia, but really it's because it makes my feet hurt and is inordinately expensive. Besides, I usually get cornered by some crasher who wants to talk about art or music or something, and I never really want to do that, especially not in a high-pitched scream and on the hoof.

I know one person who I always considered had the social graces of a wart-hog, but I'm beginning to disapprove of him less. I think he's really quite sensible. Faced with the prospect of boredom, he doesn't even attempt to converse but eats everything in sight, hoovering his way through the olives and crisps and quite possibly finishing off with the chrysanthemums. Then he goes home to sleep, having had a (sort of) free meal and not having sung for it at all.

My beloved Rosamond was at a party the other evening where all the chairs had been roped off. Nothing daunted, she went and sat in one, but in the meantime she had unwarily accepted a snack from a tray and it had turned out to be a lobster claw. So there she was stuck with the beastly thing and nowhere to dispose of it. I have a shamefaced feeling that if it had been me I would have pushed it down the side of the chair, but luckily Rosamond's grandson was also present and he relieved her of it. It didn't end there, however, because he couldn't think what to do with it either, and she could see him debating with himself whether to sling it in the pool which graced the centre of the room. These problems do nothing to enhance the quality of life.

The quality of life is not of the highest at the moment anyway. We are all suffering from the lack of ultra-violet rays which have been in short supply all year and everybody has a glum, grey look and a tendency to crack at the smallest thing. Our judgement is impaired. Mine is, anyway. Faced with the problem of what to wear to parties on top of the easily creased little frocks one wears underneath, I bought myself a coat of quite spectacular vulgarity from a stall in the market. It is mock snow-leopard, and the third son remarked that I should consider the quantity of nylon sacrificed to go into its construction. Still, at least no one else is tempted to borrow it.

The daughter recently mislaid a brand new coat and insists that the last time she saw it her father was wearing it. Everyone in this family is always wearing everyone else's coat, but I can't really see Someone in his daughter's school gear. He himself has lost about 25 coats over the course of our acquaintance, leaving them in buses and trains and restaurants and other people's houses and managing to retain only a dreadful frayed old thing which even the local winos would not be tempted to borrow; yet despite this we are, to coin a phrase, very overcoated. There are dozens of the things in this house and I don't know where most of them came from. I am reluctant to bundle them all off to Oxfam in case their owners come back for them but am going to choose a date later in the year when the ultra-violet rays have improved my resolution and no one is likely to freeze to death, and then I shall give them all away.

In the meantime we are using the perfectly good bicycle which suddenly appeared in the garden, and I am going to wear the smart white trousers which I found in my wardrobe when I was hunting for something to wear to a party and which I have never seen before in my life. Mysteriously acquiring things is even more puzzling than losing them, though less annoying.

I'm supposed to go to two parties tonight and I wish I could say that I was going to wear my new trousers and go on the bicycle, thereby saving the taxi fare, but I never learned to ride a bicycle, considering it undignified, so I think I'll have an early night.

Foot fault

I bought some comfortable shoes the other day: white moccasin-type things with fringed tongues, and flat as a pancake. Alfie hates them to such an extent that he has become quite unbalanced on the subject. Whenever we meet, his eyes go straight to my feet and, should I happen to be wearing them, he starts clawing at the air and invoking the Deity.

'You look like a Third World person,' he says. 'You look as though you'd found them on a tip where another Third World person had thrown them away. You look like a *Peruvian*,' he adds despairingly.

He says the very sight of them makes him go all *limp* and *leffargic* and puts him off his lunch and the prospect of work and, by implication, the whole of the human race.

Alfie is very sensitive. He sank to the floor the other day, moaning about my shoes. He says he wouldn't mind so much if they were only black and, if I would just go and buy a bottle of dye (he was too weak to move), he would paint them for me. I sometimes find peoples' hats unbearably annoying, but I can't remember shoes having this effect on me.

I'm stiff feeling pretty leffargic myself. I've been explaining to everyone that the cold was rendering me incapable of all forms of work, but when the sun came out last Sunday I didn't feel galvanized a bit. The other day, in the house of my friend the analyst, where I go to work, I was overwhelmed by weariness and went to sleep instead, sharing my couch with the cat Focus who, his master says, has to have a kip in the afternoon in order to get into shape for the night's sleep. But then all the cats I know get up at 5 a.m. and clump around wondering when the lazy bastards are going to wake and give them their breakfast. Cadders and Puss stand outside the bathroom going miaow and occasionally slapping and scratching at the door. Their importunity quite spoils one's concentration as one lies in the bath plotting a novel and listening to Ken Bruce on the wireless. Sometimes a black snake-like paw insinuates itself under the door and you feel like someone in a James Bond movie where naked people are always being menaced by reptiles and tarantulas and odd-looking foreign chaps.

The daughter and I are taking an unprecedented Easter break and leaving the rest of the family to cook their own Easter bunny. We are going to Scotland, and it has just dawned on me that this involves sitting in a car for 14 hours: I never recognize unpleasant facts until I can see the whites of their eyes, but this one is doing nothing for my metabolic rate. We are travelling overnight and I'm tired already. What car games can one play with a child in total darkness? We shall have to tell jokes: 'What do you call a nun with a washing machine on her head?' 'Sister Matic.' 'Why are elephants grey and wrinkled and huge?' 'Because if they were little and round and white they'd be aspirins.' She knows some very rude ones too but I'll spare you those. I have toyed with the idea of asking a vet for a few tranquillizing darts, but I suppose we will have to rely on a plentiful supply of Smarties. I do detest travelling.

We have been instructed to bring the minimum of luggage to the Isle of Arran since the car is alarmingly minute, and this means heart-rending decisions, together with shrewd predictions as to what the weather will be doing – always problematic at this time of year. Is it worse to have only tweeds and great hairy woollies while the sun beams from a cloudless sky, or only pretty little cotton frocks while the north-easterlies roar in from the ocean? One thing is sure.

I'm taking my comfortable white shoes, and sucks to you, Alfie.

PS: I shouldn't have written that, because Alfie has just walked in, peered under the table to ascertain what I've got on my feet and gone completely mad: 'Get those effing shoes off,' he said. 'They make you look like ten bob's worth down King's Cross.' Then he tore them from my feet and put them in the bin liner.

Tales of Tiny Ted

Recently I've been reading a diary that my father kept when he was 16. My cousin Penny in Liverpool found it when she was going through her mother's effects, and now I have an odd feeling that I know the young John Lindholm better than I knew him when he got to be my Papa. He died 25 years ago, but here he is in his diary noting, on 12 March 1917: 'Get weighed in gym. Capture of Baghdad. Win colours.' On the 13th he used blanks for the first time in manoeuvres and saw an aeroplane, and on the 15th he writes: 'Palgrave has a fit in chapel. I go to music practice.' On Palm Sunday the poor darling went 'into sick-room after walk. Miss morning chapel. Paint my tooth with iodine.'

The past is quite extraordinary. I know he's dead because I sat with him while he died, but on the other hand he is *not*. I think it is most likely that our dead aren't nearly as far away as Scotland. A year or so ago I was grizzling to my friend Patrice, who is highly psychic, that I felt lousy and horrible and miserable, and wasn't life hell; and she said not to worry, my father was with me. I more or less sighed and said, 'Oh yeah, pull the other one,' and things like that, and she suddenly said, 'Who's Tiny Ted?' Now, I have to explain that, while I utterly despise those idiots who keep and exhibit their teddy bears, I have also kept mine. I never, never was so winsome as to talk about them. I would not have dreamed of doing such a thing *But* they were all tucked away in cupboards, except for Tiny Ted, who is two inches high and reclines in my underwear drawer. He formed a tremendous

bond between me and my father who was away throughout the war and used to write me weekly stories about the adventures of this bear, and had I been required to test the identity of someone claiming to be my dad by asking one question, I would have asked what Tiny Ted was up to. I swear to you that no one in the world knew of the continued existence of that bear. I kept him (and the rest) a secret from the children, because he was too frail to be abandoned to their tender mercies, and I hadn't given him a thought for years.

Reminded of these infantile matters, I then went to check on the larger bears who were in a cupboard in the laundry, only to discover that Jane had comprehensively died. I think it must have been the damp. She had disintegrated into her constituent parts and had the fearful appearance of some-body who has just been disinterred – as indeed she had. Now sentiment took over. I could not bear (*bear!*) to bung her in the bin liner, so Zélide gave me a shoe-box and I laid Jane out in it, and my friend the analyst dug a hole under a tree in Wales, and I buried her.

I favour burial over cremation, partly because I am very fond of graveyards and headstones and the peace that attends them, but I was pleasantly surprised the other day to discover that crematoriums too are relaxing places to spend an afternoon. One of my favourite neighbours, name of Dickie, took me to Golders Green to see the crocuses for a special treat, and as the sun was out and the birds were singing, we wandered round the lawns and the ponds, and I had the most enjoyable time I have had since I was last in the country. We looked at the tablets set in the walls commemorating the dead and noted how wives seemed almost invariably to have outlived husbands who were universally dearly loved and sadly missed. Not a word of acrimony, not a dissonant note. We saw a bust of Ivor Novello (best profile forward) and were astonished (though I don't quite know why) to discover that Wilhelmina Stitch had also ended up there. Perhaps the argument of cremation $v.$ burial is in the same class as the argument as to whether the milk should go in the tea last or first – not wildly important. We ended our visit by having tea in a tiny building, grandly described as The Refectory. It was painted in Thirties pink-and-blue and divided into two sections – one for staff and one for mourners – and was wonderfully reassuring with motherly waitresses. I had a delicious scone and a cup of tea – milk in first.

Mixed blessings

I don't want to go on and on about the weather but when it's hanging on your eyelashes in the form of snow, or blasting up your sleeves in the shape of a Force 9 gale, it's quite difficult to think about anything else. We were really rather lucky in Scotland. The wind admittedly was such that it would blow the earrings out of your ears were they not well tucked back in the hood of your duffel coat, but when it wasn't snowing, sleeting, hailing or raining the sun beamed on the ocean and the ocean beamed back; and ensconced in a sheltered corner under the house wall, wrapped in the aforementioned duffel, it was possible to drink one's morning coffee before it froze over.

The daffodils nodding dizzily on the lawn were the tiny, wild kind, as became apparent when one, more daring then its fellows, stripped off its green coating to brave the gusts and torrents and revealed itself simply, palely yellow. I wonder what it is about daffodils that inclines people to carry on like that. Only the wild kind have this effect. I don't think Wordsworth was addressing himself to the big butch sort with orange middles that look like fried eggs on stalks. I was awfully tempted to give the daughter a lecture about fields of asphodel: only I couldn't remember anything except that boring old Greek ghosts used to gibber round in them. At least I think they did. I thought better of it too, because she was sleeping up in the attic and the mention of ghosts seemed inadvisable. I did tell her that after Ailsa Craig came Ireland and after that America, and I hope I got it right, not really being qualified to teach anybody anything. I wished I had heeded Janet more closely, because she is quite expert on the subject of which bird is which and there were all sorts bobbing about on the sea and flying around in the air and eating crumbs in the garden. We saw a gannet and a cormorant and some oystercatchers and a robin, which are fairly easy to identify, and two starlings came down the chimney in my bedroom. I got to know them quite well before one of my hosts collared them and put them out of the window.

We took the daughter to Hatfield House the other day to watch her father playing tennis, and when we'd done that for a while we went on a guided tour of the house, mostly because it was warmer in there. It was much like every other Stately Home, with stairs and galleries and horribly uncomfortable-looking furniture, and a photograph of the Queen Mother (signed) on an occasional table, and portraits of the family, together with various knick-knacks acquired over the years. There was one very, very nasty painting of a countess, done by Cecil Beaton. It must have been then, Janet and I concluded, that he had wisely decided to take up the camera.

Janet is a mixed blessing on these occasions. She is fairly sound on history and can quote chunks of Shakespeare, which are quite appropriate when one is confronted with a picture of Gloriana on a horse claiming to have the heart and stomach of a king (which makes me think of haggis, especially when I've just got back from Scotland); but she can let the side down. Standing in an imposing room amidst a number of hushed tourists, we were listening to a scholarly exposition by the guide on its merits and interesting points when her attention wandered to the fireplace. It was ornately carved with figures and plants and ribbons and represented, I suppose, some mythical event from Classical times. 'Pssst,' said Janet, addressing me by name in an audible whisper. 'Why has that cherub got his hand up that lady's bunch of flowers?' He had too. And *I* don't know why. The bouquet was judiciously poised in the position occupied by the fig leaf in Christian legend, and I didn't hear much more of what the guide was telling us because I was speculating. Perhaps the sculptor couldn't carve hands very convincingly. They are terribly difficult to paint and the temptation is often to leave them in pockets or behind the back. Maybe he had just been lazy. Maybe there was an even simpler explanation and this was yet one more of the stories I had forgotten. Perhaps her suspender had snapped. Then I began to wonder how many dignitaries ranged at this fireside sipping Buck's Fizz or some other aristocratic beverage had had their eyes caught by this unedifying cherub, and what their reactions had been.

'Now,' I finally heard the guide saying, 'does anyone have a question they would like to ask me?' If I had been a worse person I would have turned to Janet and said very loudly, 'I think you have, haven't you, darling?' but I restrained myself and now I don't suppose we'll ever know.

Uncommon courtesy

I think people have forgotten how to be easily polite. Americans over here overdo it (I don't know how they behave back home) and a lot of us don't do it at all, blowing on our soup and neglecting to pass the salt. Italian waiters overdo it as well. It is difficult to appreciate one's lasagne properly with a pair of them bowing and scraping at you like windscreen wipers. They are not much less annoying than the opposite sort who find you invisible until you show signs of leaving without paying the bill.

There is a maxim that to be seen on a bus after the age of 40 is a sign of failure, but this is not the reason I so seldom avail myself of public transport. The reason is that the bus never comes and when it does the conductor is almost invariably unhelpful and the public jostle you. Someone says one of the most maddening things in the world is to be bumped into by some clodhopper who doesn't know the rules. Being a gent, he himself always says (despite tottering from the onslaught) 'Sorry', and the proper response to this on the part of the jostler is also 'Sorry'. Too often the actual response is more like 'Well, okay, but don't do it again', or worse, 'Why don't you bloody look where you're going?' Now wonder there is so much violence on the streets.

A little while ago I had cause to visit the *Spectator* offices. We drove triumphantly into Doughty Street which on previous occasions we have failed to locate, and Janet said, 'Right, what's the number?' and I said I'd forgotten and she said something and we drove up and down in the hope that I would recognize the building; but the houses in Doughty Street are like people of a race different from your own in that they are impossible to tell apart, and while I could see the houses quite clearly and even read the numbers on them, I couldn't see the small print on the various plates, and anyway, as we discovered later, the *Spectator* doesn't have one.Then I saw a red notice saying, in large letters, 'Social Services', so, relieved, we stopped in the car and I popped in through the welcomingly open door.

There were two ladies there, one old and one young, sort of leaning against the filing cabinets.

'Do you happen to know,' I enquired very politely, 'the number of the *Spectator* offices?'

'No,' said the old one.

'Then could you look it up for me in your telephone book?' I asked, still very polite.

'No,' said the young one.

'We haven't got time,' said the old one.

'Then could I borrow your telephone book and look it up myself?' I asked.

It took the old one a few seconds to counter this but she rallied finally. 'There's a pile behind you,' she said. 'Try that.'

Turning, I discovered that there was indeed a pile – about three feet high – of pink telephone books E – K. I left.

To be fair there was also a young man with them who looked – like a good German – as though he would like to help if he dared but knew that it was more than his life was worth. Except for me there wasn't a single member of the public within miles of the place.

As we were ambling pointlessly up and down Doughty Street, the young man sneaked up after us with a muttered apology delivered surreptitiously from the side of his face, behind his hand. 'Try the public telephone over there,' he whispered, not looking at us. Then he walked swiftly away, glancing neither right nor left.

Delighted to note this redeeming feature in the human race we hastened to the telephone box, but it contained no telephone directories. They had obviously been stolen, not because the thief desired them, but because it was a jolly good way to discommode the public.

We were about to go home, thoroughly disenchanted, when we saw, through a window, a lady with her head bent over a deskful of papers. The sign on the door said 'Printers Benevolent Society,' and we decided to give the human race one more chance.

'You go this time,' I said to Janet.

I was fed up with being snubbed and waited hopelessly on the pavement expecting to hear that the word should have read Malevolent; but no. After a while Janet emerged with a spring to her step and the number of the *Spectator* offices on her lips. The lady had looked it up in her telephone book without a moment's hesitation, putting aside her workload without demur, and she had even smiled.

Gina wasn't at all cross with us for being late and we left feeling much better, but sometimes in the watches of the night I wonder what bitter experience could have soured the natures of those two ladies so dreadfully.

C'est la vie

I woke up on the wrong side of the bed today in a filthy mood before I had even swung the legs over the side. It is the weekend – with not just a bloody Sunday, but a bloody

Saturday, to get through before the peaceful shores of Monday morning heave into view through the mist. I voiced a few thoughts as I lay looking out at the rain falling on Camden Town and Someone asked tenderly what he could do to make my life more interesting, whereupon I reminded him of the old Chinese curse: smiling inscrutably, they say to anyone they've really got it in for, 'May you have an interesting life.' What I want is a few years of uninterrupted boredom. The possibility that the smell in the linen cupboard is redolent of dry rot is extremely fascinating; the chance that the sapling, which seeded itself in the garden and grew virtually unnoticed, has now got a death grip on the drains is most diverting; and I bet not many people have Colorado beetle in their bedrooms.

The fifth son complained. 'Mum, these little bugs keep jumping on me.'

'Cat fleas?' I suggested. 'Snake ticks?'

'No,' he said thoughtfully, 'they're about so big, and they're yellow with black stripes.'

Do I alert the council pest-exterminator, or the Ministry of Agriculture? Do I care? When life is as interesting as this, one tends to get blasé.

Perhaps fearing that time might be lying heavily on my hands, this same son left a heap of camping equipment on the dining-room floor, when he returned from a weekend of Battle Re-enactment. I ignored it for some time until one day, sitting discussing life with a neighbour, we noticed a powerful smell of gas. Hastily we rang the gas board and a silent man duly appeared with a great deal of gas-discerning equipment. Neither this nor his own olfactory sense proved anything to be amiss and he left, still silent and by now also rather scornful. *Women* was the message evident from his body language. The fact that the whole house still stank of gas seemed not to have registered on him or anything. It was, of course, upon Janet that the truth finally dawned.

Whisking aside a sleeping-bag she discovered a leaking canister of camping gaz which had flipped its lid. 'I wondered what the smell was,' observed the son when I mentioned this to him. Talk about Battle Re-enactment.

My recent reading has done nothing to improve my conceit of myself. I have been learning about the African martyrs of 1885 and have been forced to the realization that if anyone offered to cut out the sinews of my arms and roast them in front of my eyes I should retract, apostasize, apologize, grovel without a moment's hesitation. My neighbour Gwynne suggested that this would be only sensible, and then, as one disappeared over the horizon, one could re-retract with a cry of 'Yah-boo-sucks' to one's would-be tormentors, but I don't think that's quite the point.

One way of avoiding boredom is to exchange it for the depression engendered by the contemplation of the ingenuity which human beings can bring to bear on discomfiting their fellows. I was once told about an empress of China who took a dislike to one of the court ladies: she cut her arms and legs off and packed her into a jar and kept her as a sort of pet, daily rolling her out to amuse the other courtiers. When I recounted this anecdote to my friend Jenny she was very quiet for a moment and then remarked that the awful thing was that the incident had a terrible kind of *style*.

Looking on the bright side I can only suppose that the empress must have been very, very bored. If she had had dry rot and beetles and gas leaks to contend with she wouldn't have had the time to think that one up, so I console myself with the reflection that all the irritating vicissitudes of *la vie* serve to keep us all on the straight and narrow.

'I've heard of Chinese take-aways,
but this is ridiculous!'

Pig tales

Someone is thrilled to bits with his latest publication. It is entitled *The History of the British Pig* and is by Julian Wiseman and I have to confess that, for reasons I cannot precisely put my finger on, it *is* rather compelling. I have never previously given much thought to the pig, being aware of him only as a balding pink creature with a curly tail, teetering around in muck on little high-heeled hooves. I have rubbed oil and salt into his skin to make his crackling crisp, and I have grown as annoyed as everyone else to find that the manufacturers have somehow contrived to introduce a great deal of water into his bacon so that it sticks to the pan which consequently has to be scoured before you can fry the eggs in it. I have also retained in my mind for years a piece of probably untrue, and certainly useless, information to the effect that chocolate is poison to pigs and if found in their swill will cause them to drop down dead. As I detest waste I was cross to learn some years ago of the abandonment of the scheme whereby what people left on their plates in various canteens and institutions was scraped into bins to be converted into swill for these omnivorous animals. I used to worry vaguely sometimes, when I couldn't think of anything else to worry about, that the remains of a Mars bar or a cup of cocoa might inadvertently be included by some ignorant person and cause mayhem in the piggeries. I knew, like everyone else, that every bit of the pig, apart from the squeak, was of use to mankind, and I have heard that it is very painful to be bitten by one. But then being bitten by anything isn't very nice.

Apart from all that, I was content to let the pig go his way while I went mine. No longer. The pig is a peculiarly fascinating beast, and now that I have broken my silence on the subject, I have been astonished at the numbers of people who have long held this view.

Wherein then lies the appeal? Perhaps, I muse, it arises from the ambivalence which mankind feels towards this animal. In the introduction to *The History of the British Pig* the author quotes one John Mills as follows:

> Of all the quadrupeds that we know, or at least certainly of all those that come under the husbandman's care, the Hog appears to be the foulest, the most brutish, and the most apt to commit waste wherever it goes. The defects of its figure seem to influence its dispositions: all its ways are gross, all its inclinations are filthy, and all its sensations concentrate in a furious lust, and so eager a gluttony, that it devours indiscriminately whatever comes in its way.

Help. It seems particularly unfair to cast aspersions on the pig's figure, since an illustration of the common pig of Europe shows him to be as slim as you could wish and it is undoubtedly the hand of man that has fattened the hog.

Having devoured *The History* of same I looked eagerly round for further reading and was handed by Someone *The Book of the Pig*, a 19th-century work crammed with the misleading scientific information so dear to the Victorians, and full of the most amazing pictures – some of which also appear in the book under discussion. I particularly recommend the drawing of two Poland Chinas; they are *all* solid pig with teensy little snouts and weensy little legs and look exactly like two dirigibles – as remote from the wild boar as the Pomeranian from the wolf. Then there is the print dated 1809 showing a chap in a hat with a sow about ten times his size. Artistic licence, you think to yourself. But no. There it

61

A practically circular pig circa 1796

is in black and white: 'This pig weighed 12 cwt at four years of age.' Below that is a picture of a practically circular pig which, observes the author, was, at 802 lbs live weight, by no means the largest recorded. He isn't kidding. Turning to my other source I read that 'in America . . . a hog was exhibited which reached the marvellous weight of 1325 lb'. That is one hell of a lot of pork chops. By this time the gentry had taken over the breeding of the pig. Left to himself and without the help of such as Lord Emsworth, the peasant would have been content with his little pig of no particular breed rootling round in his backyard, or foraging in the woods (this was called pannage and the peasant had to pay for it). Now we have all sorts of pigs – black, white, mottled, spotted, saddled, sheeted, razor-backed, lop-eared, everything the heart could desire. At least, I think we have. Some of them might have died out again, and I haven't seen a live one for ages except at a distance. Now that my interest has been kindled I am determined to make closer acquaintance with this underrated beast.

Ringing tones

Alfie was in his sister Marion's house the other day when the telephone rang.

'Ooh,' she cried, jumping a foot in the air and dropping a plate. 'You answer it, Alfie.'

'Hullo,' said Alfie, and the other person asked how long the sessions lasted and what they cost. '*Pardon?*' said Alfie.

Marion said the phone had hardly stopped ringing all day and half the male population of London seemed to be under the impression that she offered specialized massage at a reasonable rate. It turned out that the printers had inadvertently transposed two telephone numbers in an ad in the local paper and this was the result.

I rather hate the telephone, especially the new sort which makes an awful kind of chirrup like a demented bird. I can never think what on earth it is when it suddenly starts cheeping, and it is maddening when you bother to answer it only to find that you have a lunatic on the other end who maintains a determined and – inevitably – rather threatening silence. Dirty phone calls are unpleasant but at least you have some vague idea of the maniac's motives. I can see no rhyme or reason in ringing somebody's number in order not to say *anything*. Is it burglars? I am also irritated when the man who tells you the time goes on to say what watch he's telling it you by. I really don't want to know that. All I want is the correct time, unadorned. I am in two minds about the telephone, actually. It does save one from having to write letters and enables one to talk at length to one's friends but, being temperamentally inclined towards pessimism, I always fear that when I answer it I shall find myself speaking to somebody who wants money or to invite me to the opera.

Crossed lines seem less frequent than they used to be, and on the whole I'm rather sorry. I know it is disgusting to eavesdrop but I have gained some useful insights into human nature by dint of the crossed line, not least into its stupidity. A lady once rang the number she wanted and got us. We told her she'd got it wrong and she rang off. Then she tried again and got us again. This went on for longer than you would believe, and she, *she*, got very angry. 'Now, listen,' she said at about the 31st ring, 'I've asked my friend to step into the box and watch the number I'm dialling, and *this is it*.' Nothing we said could convince her that this was immaterial, that whoever it was she wanted she was getting us, and we weren't them. She was nearly speechless with fury by the end of the day.

Then I once cut in on an assignation. A lady was saying rather winsomely that she thought she might find herself in a certain spot on a certain evening and she'd have her overnight bag with her. The gentleman to whom she spoke received this intelligence with equanimity – I put it no higher, he was not breathless with excitement. Then she remarked that his kiddies were home early, she could hear them in the background, and there was a rather terrible hush. 'Those are *your* kiddies,' he uttered at last. 'Mine are still at school.' At this there was another moment's appalled silence and then both parties hung up with a simultaneous crash. The kiddies who were screeching in the background were mine, the party of the third part. I felt I had put an end to a clearly unpromising adulterous liaison, and less guilty than I should have done. I also felt sorry that I hadn't thought to claim to be the voice of God just reminding them of the seventh commandment. It must be marvellous fun ticking people off when they don't know where you are, concealed in the mists of Mount Sinai.

The telephone is bound to ring again in a minute and I'm wondering what I'll say if it's God.

Ash, no sackcloth

The telephone continues to baffle me. I came home the other day to find a message from Maureen. She had been dusting the drawing room when the lunatic thing rang and told her to tell me that my brother in Australia was returning my call and would ring again that evening. 'Oh good,' I thought, and it took me a moment to remember that I don't have a brother – in Australia or anywhere else. I am an only child, although my mother occasionally appears to forget this too. Sometimes when I ring her I say, 'Hullo Mummy', and she says, 'Is that you darling?'

Being so solitary I was enchanted to discover the other day that my cousin Jeffrey (no relation, if you follow me – I wondered for a while whether it was my fate to dote on men called Jeffrey, and then I remembered Mrs Thatcher's one) and I are exactly alike – well, not exactly. You could tell us apart, but he and I are very similar. For one thing he smokes and drinks, and when told by people shaking their heads mournfully that he will not reach a ripe old age he says he doesn't give a toot: my sentiments entirely. I often think, when it's raining and the telephone doesn't stop ringing, that if the Grim Reaper were to lean over the garden wall beckoning with a bony digit, I would slip my tiny hand trustfully in his and go off with him without a backward glance. In passing: I was told recently by an economist, who presumably has a good grasp of numbers, that there are now more people alive than there are dead – that the great majority is now the minority. Can this be true? How does he know? How many angels can dance on the point of a pin?

But to return to my cousin Jeffrey. He loves cooking. He spends hours in the kitchen smoking and drinking and making elaborate Chinese meals for his wife and children, and then he doesn't eat any of it himself. I do that too. I like everyone to sit down at a table out of my way while I hover about in the back kitchen with the fags. Guests, of course, find this rather disconcerting, and I can see why. It is not reassuring to reflect that the *patron* doesn't *mange ici*, but I promise everyone the food is perfectly wholesome and there isn't even any fag ash in it, because us confirmed smokers are adept at holding the left, fag-bearing, hand well out of the way. My cousin smokes in the bath and can wash his hair with one hand, and I have developed a method of flicking the ash down my sleeve when I find myself marooned in the middle of a room surrounded by people with the ashtray miles out of reach on a corner table. The butt presents a problem, though; now so many people are straining after Health, a lot of them leave their drinks half drunk, and a glass with a bit of white wine in it offers a safe means of disposal and is less offensive to the host than burn-holes in the Axminster, I think. I was once asked to a party by some Americans who wrote on the invitation: 'This is a non-smoking household.' I didn't bother to reply. Could they have imagined that I would prefer to be with them rather than sitting in my kitchen, smoking?

I find some people's thought-processes awfully difficult to follow. Not least those of my friend the analyst, who has just telephoned me because he wanted somebody to shout at. He was mad with three other people, but they were all out; so he went prowling round to find a legitimate cause of complaint and was grimly delighted to discover what he describes as a burn-hole in a plastic thing in his garden. He accused me of causing it by dropping a lighted cigarette-end off his flat roof, and when I indignantly denied it he said I was only making it worse by telling lies. If he will go out on to his flat roof he will find, in the wall flanking it, a hole in the pointing; and if he will look in this hole he will find that I have stuffed all the fag-ends in there.

I love most of my friends and some of my relations, but the ones I love best are visible in the dark because they have a glowing fag in their face.

Gloom and doom

It was the 13th yesterday. I have the sort of watch that isn't supposed to stop ever, and yesterday it stopped at one o'clock. It's started again since, but I didn't like it stopping. As evening drew on I glanced out of the window and espied the trimmed toenail sliver of the newest possible moon. I felt I might just as well throw a boot through a looking-glass and go out and stroll under a few ladders. I am not as rabidly superstitious as some – for instance my friend Richard who goes to fanatical lengths in order not to see the new moon through glass and will drive with his head stuck out of the car window in sub-zero conditions if the thing is imminent – but I felt a touch uneasy. My religion forbids me to give way to superstitious fears, so I swiftly said a paternoster and an ave, which is wholly illogical and not altogether sane. I also comforted myself with the thought that the window through which I saw the wretched thing was double-glazed and that this would negate the misfortune.

Our friend Bill was dashed unlucky the other day. As he was about to leave after lunch the heavens opened and I said, 'Bill, that rain is radioactive and you must be very careful and put up your umbrella or you will start glowing in the dark.' Then as he was walking through the park on his way to the tube he was struck by lightning. It zoomed in, zonk on the top of his umbrella, slid down the plastic handle and bounced off his hand. It didn't kill him, but it certainly gave him a nasty turn. All this unleashing of power makes one edgy. While the unfortunate Russians were throwing mud at their reactor, I spoke to a scientific person who seemed to think they could well be making a mistake. He explained gloomily that this might squash all the little neutrons closer together until they formed what is known as a critical mass and shot down through the earth until they hit the water table, whereupon, bang, the entire Ukraine would be rendered lethally uninhabitable for more or less *ever*. Now this was a man who, on the whole, is pleased that $E=Mc^2$, so his despondency struck chill to my heart. Discussing the earth, I was reminded that, like all the nicest things to eat, it is crispy on the outside and soft in the middle and it seems a pity if its inhabitants are going to blow it to smithereens.

The stepmother of the girlfriend of one of the sons was acting in a theatre in north Wales at the time and the warning system at the local nuclear establishment started going bleep because the level of radioactivity around had gone as high as a kite. The son was in Wales too, so I rang him up and whimpered that they mustn't drink the water and certainly not the milk because cows are wonderfully efficient at hoovering up the nasties and concentrating them, and that they must cut out the broad-leaved veg. He told me shortly not to be so silly. Humanity now seems to divide into those who refuse to worry and those who would rather starve than eat lettuce. (Anyway I read somewhere that lettuces contain positively hundreds of chemicals designed to discourage greenfly and moth and blackspot and God know what else, so already they don't sound too wholesome.)

I only wish that the experts didn't also fall on both sides of this divide. There are experts in every single field of human endeavour contradicting each other flatly, and this is dizzyingly confusing for the layman seeking only to live out his allotted span without too much hassle, or the need for profound thought and decision-making about matters which any reasonable person might think he could take for granted. The layman has a hollow feeling that none of the experts really has the remotest idea of quite what the hell he's up to. Either that or half of them are lying like carpets.

It is all very worrying and discouraging, and what makes me so mad is the thought of the trouble we went to to make sure the kiddies ate up all their greens. What, I ask myself, is the point of fussing, if some ass is going to press the wrong button and render all our care redundant (this is called human error and is almost more worrying than the prospect of a wild-eyed lunatic pressing the right button)? A poem follows:

On the whole I wish we could have been spared
The genius of the man who figured out that $E=Mc^2$.

Passing thoughts

I was standing outside the fishmonger's the other day glaring at a crab and thinking. There's no point in buying a small crab – it isn't worth the aggravation. So I was measuring it for size and also remembering the last time I bought one. There I was busily slugging it with the sharpening steel when I clouted myself on the thumb. It is amazing how badly one can hurt oneself. It couldn't have been more painful if I'd been my own worst enemy. Then I fell to speculating on the relative merits of salmon and salmon trout and wondering why I had bought salmon on the previous Friday when actually I prefer salmon trout and it's a bit cheaper. After a while my gaze wandered to a row of hanging octopuses and I pondered whether I could bring myself to clean one and chop it up and, when I had done so, whether anyone would bother to eat it.

The thought of fishfingers had just entered my mind when I was approached by a young man in an orange frock, an anorak, a woolly hat and a gold-painted nose. He was bearing a load of brightly coloured paperbacks and, distracted as I was in Piscean reverie, I had bought one before I recalled my usual mode of address to Jehovah's Witnesses, Mormons, Moonies and the like. Perhaps I thought he was a gypsy. I am never rude to gypsies in case, and I still sometimes worry about the time I went to the fair on Hampstead Heath, with the rain beating down and mud up to the knees and the kiddies whirling round in the air on various machines eating candyfloss and hot dogs the while, when a gypsy fortune teller leaned out of her caravan beckoning to me and speaking as follows: 'Oi, you lady, c'm 'ere.' I shook my head and attempted to indicate that I was in charge of all the flying children and daren't take my eyes of them for fear they disappeared down the Tunnel of Love or something. I was the only adult for miles around since the weather was so vile, so I suppose she was desperate for custom. She retired, muttering and looking pretty cheesed off, and I often wonder what she wanted to tell me.

Reading the young man's book I found some of the passages fairly impenetrable: 'In his early pastimes he appears as a householder with a golden complexion . . . He is the highest abode of peace and devotion, for the "He" silences the impersonalist non-devotees.' Eh? Nevertheless the Hare Krishna movement, of which the young man was a devotee, strikes me as not being as barking mad as some of the cults. The book rather charmingly ends with an invitation to 'participate in the famous transcendental festival of chanting, mantra meditation, philosophical discussion and sumptuous vegetarian feast'.

This reminded me of the time Patrice took me to see a guru in West Hampstead. He did the cooking while two of his lady friends sat down and talked to us. The sitting down had to be done on cushions on the floor, which made me bad-tempered. Then he joined us wearing a dress which buttoned (more or less) up the front and no knickers and he talked a lot of the most frightful old cobblers which made me worse tempered; but what made me hopping mad was that we got water to drink while he downed a couple of buckets of curaçao. In the end I *demanded* that he give me some too, and after a glass or three I told him he was a charlatan and Patrice too me home, vowing never to take me anywhere ever again.

Despite being fearsomely ugly he kept on swanking about how wonderful he was in bed while his lady friends fluttered round pretending not to mind each other. He wasn't just

71

horrible and a lousy cook and a hopeless host – he was a crashing bore. I do not understand how these nutty gurus acquire fleets of Rolls Royces and hordes of fat-headed followers longing to sign away their fortunes. I know dozens of perfectly delightful RC priests who can not only offer guidance and insight into centuries of spiritual awareness and make sense, but can converse amusingly over the dinner table and then go home on their bikes or get on the tube. Perhaps they are too dull. Perhaps if they, and the C of E chaps too, were to paint their noses gold the churches would all fill up again. They might even be able to afford to mend the roofs.

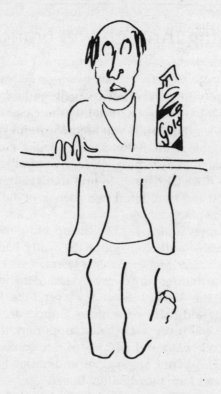

"let us spray"

Leafing through wet branches

It is notoriously difficult to burn a book; unless subjected to intense heat the outside chars while the closely compacted pages remain untouched. If you are not careful you can have the same trouble with flaky pastry. Books are, however, sadly susceptible to drowning. We arrived in the country for the first time since Christmas to find that yet another bloody pipe had burst and inundated two shelves of the only decent volumes in the place.

There are rows and rows of beat-up old paperbacks and easily replaceable anthologies but the water had unerringly made for the *Reader's Bible*, *Platonis Opera*, a set of Thackeray (particularly irritating since my friend Amanda – Young Journalist of the Year, bless her clever little heart – had recently suggested that I read him – authors are like football teams and I was ever a Dickens supporter), *Harmsworth's Universal Encyclopaedia* and all sorts of nice books like Samuel Smiles's *Self-Help*. They are sagging and buckled and covered in white fur and I am inordinately upset.

My first instinct was to put them out of their misery and bury them deep in the ash pit, but I found I couldn't bring myself to do so. It isn't actually raining at the moment so I have put the poor sufferers outside in the air. They will never be their old selves on the shelves but most of them are still legible and therefore not ready for euthanasia.

I am not anthropomorphic about books but I was thinking about them just before I woke up and seeing them in terms of trees. The spine is the trunk, the pages the branches and the words the little leaves. I think the vicissitudes of life have finally driven me mad. While I was still asleep I was telling myself that technological progress is destroying one aspect of our love life. When we slapped the horse on the rump and more or less told him to go off and get extinct, except as a pet, we lost a whole huge relationship. I know some men are potty about their cars but there is no reciprocity. No one could love a tower block the way we loved small old houses. I am never going to know the girl on the check-out counter long enough to grow to love her the way I loved the grocer who used to tell me what the neighbours were up to while he sliced the bacon precisely the way I wanted it, and I know I would never weep because the computer had got wet.

We impoverish ourselves. No dammit, I won't say ourselves. I will put the blame on those of us who, impelled partly by a desire to spin a swift buck and partly by a lethal urge to meddle and fiddle and see what would happen if they twiddled a few rods a different way, are bringing us all to the edge of everlasting night. Ooh, I am cross. It isn't just nuclear fission. It's the octopoid supermarket and Swiss-type chalets on the edges of Welsh forests, and acid rain and crimplene and formica and the new-type Mass.

I must calm myself, I am about to renew my acquaintance with the horse since the daughter has expressed a desire to go pony-trekking and this has made me think of my friend Patrice. Patrice is a perfectly enchanting person but horses hate her and Paris wants to kill her. She was walking down a country lane one day when a horse stuck its head through a hedge and bit off a mouthful of her PVC mac; then she went to a race meeting with a friend who owned a placid, armchair-type horse who inexplicably danced and sidled and rolled its eyes until she returned to the refreshment tent. Still not having tumbled to the message, she was once, while pregnant, persuaded to climb on the back of the horse of Savador Dali, one Diabolo, who was very, very old and hadn't galloped for about seven years. At the touch of Patrice he broke into an amble, and then a canter, and he was off. Everyone flew after them, worried silly – not, says Patrice, about her pregnancy but about the senile Diabolo who did in fact immediately afterwards die. Then one day she was alone in a field when a herd of horses gathered about her and she had to climb a tree. She can't remember how she got out of that one and I sometimes wonder whether she's still up there and my Patrice is a doppelgänger.

Paris is even more peculiar. She says it's quite all right as long as she's crawling round in the gutter, but should she roll up looking elegant in, say, Les Deux Magots, it turns nasty. It is, she says, as though an invisible ravening beast was hurtling down the Champs Elysées intent on her destruction. If she has been invited there to discuss a film contract or a play, Paris will make quite sure that she finds herself rejected and humiliated. Walking the boulevards she is assailed by nameless terrors; and it always makes her sick. Once on the train and 12 minutes out of there she recovers and, conversely, arriving in the best of health at the Gare du Nord she instantly begins to feel seedy. If she stays away, Paris ensures that she is visited by some Parisienne bearing peculiarly malevolent Parisian viruses. She says she can only think she must have done something awful there in a previous incarnation.

The Public Lending Right computer delivered the final straw. Her latest book is called *Albany Park*, and what did it say on the PLR form? 'Albany *Paris*'.

Drowned in the wind

Four intrepid equestriennes rode up the stony ravine to emerge on the mountain top – and then we nearly got blown off our ponies. I said last week I thought I'd gone mad and now I have hard evidence. Janet was fixing up a pony-trekking expedition for the daughter and her friend Amber, and being a responsible and courageous nanny she said – albeit with some reluctance – that she would go too; and then I heard this voice saying, 'Well, I think I will as well.' That was me. Janet was absolutely astounded although not as astounded as I was myself. I was 16 when I last clambered on a horse, and in a great many years it has never occurred to me as a good idea to repeat the experience. I used to have a horrible pony, whose delight it was to throw me when I least expected it – over hedges, into ditches, on the sand, in the sea. She accepted loud noises with equanimity and regarded articulated lorries with cool composure, but she hated discarded cigarette packets and little tiny bits of sea-weed. Janet was only thrown once – at her first lesson. They said that she must immediately get back on the horse or her fear would take on neurotic proportions and she would never ride again, and she said that as far as she was concerned if she didn't see another poxy horse for a million years it would be far too soon. Considering all this I think we must both have taken temporary leave of our senses.

We set off bright and early for the stables. I was sulking because they wouldn't let me wear my old jodhpurs on the ground that they were out of style, and it seemed pointless to have kept them all this time. Janet was talking about last wills and testaments and saying things to the effect that if martyrdom was inevitable all one could do was to accept it with a good grace; and even down in the valley a great gale was blowing. This, however, was as a mere zephyr to the gale we encountered on the mountain top. Not only were we nearly blown off the horses, the horses were nearly blown off the mountain. It was like drowning in wind and none of us had a chance to give way to nerves or the vapours. *My* one (naturally) was frightened of discarded cigarette packets and plastic bags, Janet's one was enuretic, the daughter's one was plain disobedient, and Amber's one liked playing in water; we waited for some time while it stood in a stream splashing with its foreleg and clearly determined to go no further. Janet observed grimly that John Wayne never seemed to have that sort of trouble, and I reflected again how pleasant it was not to be being chased by Red Indians. I often think this when times are difficult. It's called looking on the bright side. As we clattered into the stable yard Janet remarked that we looked like the return of the Wild Hunt, and we did rather. Everyone's hair was standing on end and all the pins had been blown out of mine. Even our guide seemed a little shaken and said that there were horses in the stable who would have been round the course in ten minutes flat if they'd been faced with those gusts on the top. I think we got off lightly, though we got off the horses with as much alacrity as the stiffness would permit and retired to the pub for a soothing stirrup cup.

Back in the Welsh home everything was much as usual. Cadders opened proceedings by disembowelling a mouse on the welcome mat, and the weather was remarkably similar to last summer. All the dramas of Christmas – the snow, the ice, the floods – might never have happened. There we were with the washing steaming on the Aga and the wellies tipped up in front of it.

Janet says there is a man who forecasts the weather by

'there is a man who forecasts the weather by observing the behaviour of moles.'

observing the behaviour of moles and that he has promised us a wonderful summer. I've hardly ever seen a mole since they spend most of their time underground, but if he's right I'll join whoever it was and sit in the sun with a strawberry daiquiri toasting the little gentleman in black velvet

Station frustration

I was waiting for a train at Gospel Oak the other morning. And waiting and waiting. After a while I was deeply astonished to find myself approached by a radiant railway employee with a smile on his face. I am accustomed to railway employees with faces wearing expressions of resigned disgust as – clearly against their better judgement – they wearily sell you a ticket, or wave vaguely in the approximate direction they think your train may be coming from. This one was eager to converse. How, he asked, was I? And what a nice day, for a change, wasn't it? And where was I going? When I told him, he said cheerily that in that case I'd be better off on the opposite platform since where I was standing no trains weren't going to no Acton – they were going the other way.

Still stunned by this evidence of interest and concern, I found myself faced with yet another beaming employee bearing a sheaf of newspapers called *Leisure Express*, all about railway trains and where you can go and what you can do on them. 'I'm going to give this lady a paper,' he said. And then it became clear. 'Because,' he added, 'this is "Be Nice to the Public Week".' Ah. 'Train be along shortly,' he said and judiciously melted away.

Fifty minutes later I became aware of a disturbance further down the platform. A well-dressed gentleman of respectable mien had flung his paper to the ground, was obviously only just restraining himself from jumping up and down on it, and was uttering a bad word. Then he started pacing and muttering and rolling his eyes heavenwards, and I stood well out of his way reading my own *Leisure Express*. He was obviously longing to do someone a mischief and the station staff had gone away – perhaps to be nice to somebody else. I also felt rather inclined to bite, but I reasoned that I couldn't blame my new friends for the tardiness of the train, since they were here. Whoever was responsible was some crumb, miles away down the line.

My paper did little to relieve the frustration of this pro- longed wait. The phrase 'Alton Towers: Fun for everyone' occurring on the cover fills me with gloom. I know what that means. It means fun for the little ones if they happen to be the extrovert type who like that sort of stuff (and it is surprising how many children don't) and hell for everyone else. Sure enough I turn to the centre pages and am confronted by a picture of a family – two children, Mummy, and, rather oddly, what looks like two Daddies, careering down a waterfall in what appears to be a large slipper. The people whose faces are visible are laughing, but one of the Daddies has his head down and I think he's being sick.

Or how about this? 'At Alton Towers the mood is ever changing' (I bet). 'If it is excitement you are after, Alton has the ultimate in "white knuckle" rides like the sensational Black Hole in Fantasy World. This pitch-dark space-ride plunges you down seemingly sheer drops and round impossibly tight bends.' I get vertigo when the train moves into Camden Town on the overhead rail. Then I read of a 'completely new themed area called Kiddies' Kingdom which is devoted entirely to younger children. Like a mini-assault course, youngsters have the time of their lives on attractions like Biff and Bash, Cookie Mountain and Tarzan Run.' I have often in my mind likened younger children to demented little paratroopers from outer space, but I have never quite seen them as an actual assault course.

Should you be feeling peckish you will be reassured to know that '. . . if you are in a hurry to get back on to the rides, the Talbot – the biggest fast-food restaurant in Europe – can feed 1,000 people an hour'. And if you're worried about germs you needn't be: 'A keen-eyed and efficient task-force preserves Alton's enviable reputation for cleanliness. The staff are neatly uniformed and have that all too rare attitude of caring for people.' Well, so they have at Gospel Oak station, but that doesn't make the trains run on time. I don't think we've got our priorities quite straight. Back to Alton Towers: 'So far the company has spent £50 million theming more than 100 attractions into the former estates of the Earls of Shrewsbury,' Poor old Earls.

Furs and furbelows

It occurred to me the other day that the inside of my wardrobe very much resembles the inside of my head; that is, it is crammed with outmoded articles, forgotten trivia and all sorts of things which I have absolutely no recollection of putting in there and cannot imagine ever using. I can't believe I ever did use some of them. Golden shoes with platform soles? My friend the analyst chanced to be here the other day and I thought that with his trained mind he might be able to prevail upon me to impose some sort of order on all that chaos. If he had been a plumber I would have led him to the washing-machine which has taken to vomiting dirty water out of the soap-powder drawer, if he had been a builder I would have shown him the course of bricks which has mysteriously fallen off the back wall, squashing the mint, and if he had been a professional baritone I would doubtless have asked him to sing. As it was, I flung open the doors (standing well back) and said, 'Behold.'

He wasn't very interested. I think his mind was elsewhere.

I leapt in at random, drew out my musquash from the wardrobe floor and it utterly came to pieces in my hands: lots and lots of horrid little pieces – tufts and gobbets and morsels, ineffably carnal, mortal and irretrievably deceased. I remember one of the cats got shut in with it some years ago and slept on it until discovered, but I had subsequently sponged it and given it a good airing and put it back to wait to be mended (it was a full-length musquash and the weight of the bottom half had caused it to drop off the top), but something, cat fleas or not, had wrought total destruction

upon it. There was no question of hesitation of 'Well, why don't we hang on to it? You never know it might come in handy. We could make a muff out of what's left.' We had to employ dust-pan and brush to get the remains into the bin bag. I then felt I had done enough for one day and delved no deeper.

I've got two more fur coats in various stages of dissolution and a mock snow leopard of such brazen artifice that it goes right the way round and is almost tasteful. All the genuine animal furs I got second-hand, which for some irrational reason makes me feel less guilty about the fate of the original owners. The threatening 'The first one to wear that coat died in it' has less force if other wearers have come between you

and it, although I never quite like to look straight in the eye of my fox fur – especially since Beryl inadvertently burned the tip of its tail off while lighting a cigarette – because I would recognize a fox if I saw one. I don't know what musquashes are. Somebody told me they were a sort of rat, but musquash was not what they were called when they were still alive and kicking, so I am no wiser. One of my other coats is reddish blonde with vague stripes; of roughish, harsh texture, it is reminiscent of hyena. It isn't lion or tiger but looks as though it came off a largish animal since the stripes go on quite far, and we are all mystified. I once had a neighbour with a coat made of cow skin, and while I feel only a fanatic would complain about that, since cows are always having their skins turned into shoes or club arm-chairs, I felt she was nonetheless taking a chance. Stepping unwarily in front of a passing car she would have handed the irate motorist the appropriate epithet and choice of phrase on a plate. The coat was cream-coloured with big brown splashes and could have belonged to absolutely nothing but a cow.

My third fur coat used to belong to my aunt and is also unrecognizable – dark brown and faintly lustrous. It is obviously genuine fur, but of what we cannot tell. I lent it to Zélide last winter to keep her warm when she went off researching marine matters in Holland and as she left for home her colleagues told her she was lucky no animal rights protesters had thrown eggs at her (do eggs have no rights?). I sympathize to some extent with their outrage, but I would go even further if I could discover precisely *which* animal's rights I had infringed.

Wheels within wheels

I have been thinking about wheels, and the pitfalls – or possibly potholes – they offer to those who would aspire to style. Cars, for instance. I know very little about cars although I am learning, as the years go by, more things than I wish to know: how to push them down hills when their batteries go flat, how to keep a foot on the appropriate pedal while some improvident chump fiddles about in their insides because he forgot to consult a garage mechanic before setting out – awful, boring things. I don't want to know about cars. I expect them only to keep out the rain and take me forthwith where I wish to go.

Nevertheless, people keep telling me more things about them. I learn that our own car – a Cortina Estate – is definitely, but definitely, naff; and I don't care. Janet drives it, and the pair of them get along perfectly well. Although, as we believe, Janet is descended from Queen Boudicca, she is a careful and considerate road-user, retaining only her ancestress's more amiable traits. Now I come to think about it I realize that I am anthropomorphic about cars – that is, the ones I am close to – and I remember the guilt I felt when we sent the present car's predecessor to the knacker's yard. It was something of a rogue car, often refusing to move when it arrived in Wales, and twice tossing up its bonnet on the motorway, but I felt pity and remorse as Janet drove it on its final journey. Common and faintly dangerous it may have been, but we had travelled far together. My latest thesis is that *all* cars are common; that now that the traffic will soon

86

be solid from coast to coast and, if we wish to progress, we shall have to walk on top of it, it is madly unusual and brilliantly chic to cross London on a 31 or 74 bus, or dive down the Underground or on to the little train that traverses the Broad Street line. A lot of people do use public transport, but not as many as drive cars. The third son holds a particular animus towards Hampstead-dwellers who bowl down the hill to avail themselves of the market fruit and veg at attractive Camden Town prices and then pile their purchases into what he describes as Hippo-mobiles, which are sort of jeeps with a picture of a rhinoceros on the spare wheel. ('Tristram [son, or husband in the case of young couples: I'm afraid the Tristrams are growing up], hold Rita [wolfhound] while I put the asparagus in the back.') Janet detests Volvos (inconsiderate and arrogant) and I have recently taken against Rolls Royces, which remind me of immensely rich, smooth and creamy abortionists. I don't quite know why this is, except that the suspicion I feel when passing a Roller is similar to the reservations that arise in me when I am introduced to an expensively dressed man with very clean fingernails and highly polished manners.

Then there are prams – or rather there aren't any more. It is years since I saw a perambulator of the old sort, highly sprung with a hood and a cover and a coat of arms on the side. Round here, certainly, all the babies are either slung over their mother's shoulders or packed in little pushchairs with transparent envelopes when it rains, so that they look like frozen chickens. When I *think* of the fuss people used to make about the spines of babies and the consistency of their pram mattresses! I had a grotty pram when we first came here. It was always crammed with kiddies at various stages of development, and a wheel kept falling off. Taking pity on us, two of the market stall-holders presented us with a very superior pram, not new but in excellent condition, and I often used to wonder, as I pushed it round, what they'd done with the baby.

Here, I think, we have a sort of social progress. It is surely impossible to construct a snobbery around prams which fold up like umbrellas. You never know, of course. Snobbery is like ground-elder, virtually ineradicable. My posher neighbours have always sneered at my shopping-basket on wheels, but the other day my friend the social worker uttered a light, incredulous laugh as he caught me outside the fishmonger's filling the aforesaid basket with herrings. 'Wheels?' he said. 'A basket on wheels?' Where did he get that from? I shall expand on this subject next week, but now I'm going to tell you something you didn't know before: used-car dealers are always grinding to a halt because, even when driving a car they may have had for 20 years, they are loth to put petrol in it in case somebody buys it in a minute, thereby also acquiring a full tank, free.

The way of the West

I watched John Wayne being chased by Red Indians yesterday afternoon. They never caught him. They never did catch him despite outnumbering him by a cast of thousands and the fact that as he got older he always reminded me of a badly packed carpet bag, lolloping along on his horse, speaking as little as possible. He must have been hell to sit next to at dinner.

But I'm not really thinking about John Wayne. Once you've thought about him for a minute or two there isn't much more to think. I'm thinking about Red Indians again. When I was a child I had a book about them. Or rather it was about some winsome white children who used to visit an old chief in his tepee to hear him tell stories, and he would roast them gobbets of game on a stick thrust over the campfire. I was reading this in wartime when it was not unknown for Sunday lunch to consist of roast Spam, and once a week school dinner was corned-beef stew. The evocation, in my Red Indian book, of fragrant tender morsels of prairie hen or chipmunk or whatever it was sizzling away over the embers and wood-smoke while the sun sank wherever it does sink in the West – even further west? – spoilt utterly the prospect of sausages (mainly bread flavoured with minced lung) for supper.

I am no longer as carnivorous as I was and I am annoyed that I seem able to remember the cooking better than the rest of the content of this book. When I was young I was completely fascinated by it. There was a lot of *Golden Bough* stuff – beautiful young yellow-haired gods bleeding to death in spots where the corn duly sprang up – although I don't know how the Red Indians conceived the idea of yellow hair before John Wayne arrived with his acolytes and women folk, and running through it were the adventures of some of those mischievous demi-gods who pop up in myths all over the place. This one spent some of his time as a wolverine – gulo gulo – and I have never since read anything half as interesting. Wolverines are terribly clever. They can dismantle traps and sometimes they sit up in the snow and shade their eyes with their paws to watch the trappers at their labours. They drive the trappers absolutely mad. If anyone should chance to recognize my book from this description and have a copy to hand will he lend it to me?

All of that has nothing to do with what I was originally going to say about Red Indians. I was going to say that they never had the problem I was exercising myself about last week – wheels, and which type are common. The Red Indian never got round to the wheel, contenting himself, if he had to take something somewhere, with lashing it on to a sort of sledge which in turn he tied to his pony. The proper name for this sledge will doubtless occur to me on Tuesday, just after this page has gone to press. His papoose was tied to his squaw and his squaw put the results of her hunter-gathering in little baskets she had made herself (no wheels). It is this business of getting the shopping home that continues to intrigue me. Is it that upper-class English ladies refuse to acknowledge that the butcher and the baker no longer call? That no longer does the head-gardener appear in the kitchen each morning with trugs full of artichokes and peas, that James is not on the drive revving up the Bugatti? Do they feel that if they admit all this and buy themselves shopping baskets on wheels they will have succumbed to vulgar fate? Do they believe that by carrying their shopping, bent double, they will somehow shame that fate into reversing itself? Yes, I think that's it. Perhaps in the meantime the poor ducks could adopt the Red Indian way and haul everything home on sledges.

The grip of the vices

Talking the other day on the telephone to my darling Caroline it suddenly occurred to me that life is very like being at sea in an open boat. ('Hang on a moment,' I said to her, 'while I just dash down this *aperçu* on the back of an envelope.') There you are rocking in the swell, awash to the gunwales as a gale recedes to westward and even the bailer has sprung a leak. You shake the maggots off the ship's biscuits, wring out your oilskins, adjust your sextant and aim at the pole only to discern yet another storm approaching inexorably over the billows. It can get very wearing. Where, you ask yourself, where the —————— is land? Trapped in this analogy, landfall must be death, I suppose. An earlier scribe, an ancient Egyptian, wrote on *his* column that life was very like a cucumber: one minute it's in your hand, and the next – well, never mind.

I only have three vices, drinking, smoking and swearing. They do something to alleviate one's time on the ocean wave, although I make occasional stabs at giving them up. Once I thought that next time I tripped on the garden steps I would remark 'Hot chocolate', but it doesn't work. It takes stronger words to relieve one's feelings and if anyone tells me that in speaking so I reveal myself as having an incomplete grasp of the English language and an inadequate vocabulary I shall spit. I have quite a wide sort of quarter-deck vocabulary and it stands me in good stead when the boat is rocking.

The other day, for instance, reading the *Guardian* column of my friend and neighbour Jill Tweedie, I learned that our part of the country – I mean the 'country': trees, grass, mountains etc – was still absolutely zizzing with radioactivity. This made me almost speechless with irritation, but I recovered and made some observations about science. We go to the country to get away, and while it is undeniable that we, in turn, come back to town in order to get away, I never foresaw this particular hazard. Floods, gales, ice, drought, the occasional mild earthquake are all inconvenient but, one feels, inevitable. What is absolutely infuriating is that there is no need for the lambs and the lettuce and the milk and God knows what else to have been rendered unwholesome. Man, with his meddling little paws, has brought that on us all by himself. Invisible death now lurks in that beautiful, holy and peaceful countryside and it really is enough to make a saint swear.

On a lesser level, there is the telephone. One of ours developed a high-pitched scream and a propensity to permit

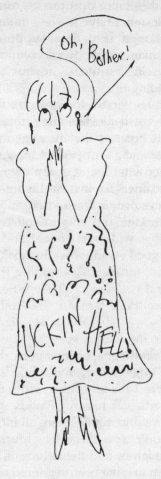

the person on the other end to hear us but not us to hear him. That gave rise to some profanity. Another one had a curiously gynaecological complaint – I think it's called inverted nipples. It refused to allow them to pop up so one could never get the dialling tone, dash it. Then the post office ran out of passport forms. Janet, whose assignment it was to pick up one of these rare documents, came back enveloped in a cerulean miasma. I have learned quite a few expressions from Janet, although she, dreadful little hypocrite, often remarks as I fall over the cat that it's *so* nice working for a *real* lady such as myself. One of the cats was out all night – Puss, the female – holding the garden against all comers. I was too tired to go down and grab her so I pulled the eiderdown over my head and called her affectionate names in silence. She's asleep in a fruit bowl at the moment together with some unanswered post and a withered plum and has scattered bits of black fluff over what remains of a novel I am working on. I discovered the other day that I had somehow mislaid about 20 uncopied pages of this work – which is quite a lot for me as I write very short novels. 'Oh *bother*,' I said.

After the party

It's when most of the guests have gone that the party really gets interesting – peering under the table and into the bath to see who's stayed and what shape they're in. It is then that those who are still conscious divulge things you had not known before: sometimes about themselves, sometimes about other people and sometimes about you. It does not necessarily make pleasant hearing but it is always fascinating. In the relaxed atmosphere, in the wake of the hubbub, they unwind and grow confidential – nay, indiscreet. If they are not already, they end up as your closest friends.

We had what I hope I may describe as a most enjoyable luncheon party yesterday. I rose at dawn to cook the potatoes and keep an eye on the sky. If it had rained it would have been catastrophic since Someone had lost count of how many people he had asked, and so had the children and so had I. It would have been like the Underground in the rush hour if we had been constrained to fit indoors. As it was, everyone went in and out and up and down the spiral staircase, clutching plates of food and glasses of wine and talking animatedly. The cats didn't like it much, but then they hadn't been invited. The daughter was a bit silent too, having just had some horrific injections in preparation for her holiday in Benin. She is also too young to drink and it is always pretty lowering being in the company of people primed with wine when you are yourself stone sober. She surveyed us rather coldly over the rim of her glass of Coke and asked me what, in view of her state of health, she could eat. 'Terrine of turkey,' I offered wildly, 'potato salad, beans in mint, spicy ham, egg mayonnaise, brie and biccies?' She declined them all and settled, I think, for a bowl of muesli followed by ice-cream.

At one stage before night fell I realized that we had some left-overs. It was tropically hot, the fridge was full and I could almost see them decaying under my nose. I made up little parcels for those who could be bothered to accept them, and then, since I cannot bear waste, I plonked a whole lot on a plastic dish and we took it down the market to give to the winos sitting under the cinema wall.

This simple, economical and charitable move gave rise to some discussion. One person was anxious lest we inadvertently found a proud wino who would throw it at us, but I thought this unlikely. Few of them are so stupid as to be proud and the food was more wholesome than the remains of the Chinese take-aways which they lift out of the municipal bins. The other school of thought arose from the Protestant view that the derelict should not be encouraged; that to those whom God loves He gives a semi-detached with a garage and an ornamental cherry in the front garden, and that those who have nothing have nothing because He

doesn't like them. If one followed this line it would of course be disrespectful to the Lord to give things to people he had chosen to reject. No one said all this in so many words but the feeling was there. I have tried but I cannot think of a single aspect of Protestantism which either appeals or makes any sense to me. I think it is only prudent to be polite to beggars because they might so easily turn out to be God or one of His angels in disguise. When the time came you might find them standing in glory at the gates of Heaven, and what would you say then?

Two old men accepted our chicken pie with grace and courtesy and I hope they enjoyed it. I never want to see another chicken pie as long as I live. Having cooked a few tons of food I don't want to see my own cooking again for a few weeks. It was fortunate for me that Jennifer brought a dish of chicken in tarragon because otherwise I might well have starved to death by now.

Washing up, I discovered an uninvited guest. Perched on the rim of a mug was a simply colossal snail. We stood blankly at each other in the gathering darkness and I don't know which of us was the more disgusted. Luckily for him I still had a grain of charity left. I gripped him firmly by his shell, detached him from the mug and slung him over the wall into my neighbour's garden.

Semi-detached

Well, here we are again in our country retreat. Nothing changes much. Cadders is asleep in the airing-cupboard and it's raining. The eldest son, who is the actual owner of Cadders, keeps exhorting him to go out and catch moles. I don't know why moles. Cadders is not a digger and moles seldom emerge from their underground fastness. I suppose he must once have caught one by inadvertence and made his master very proud. What he usually does is catch shrews and bring them inside the house where he can play with them in peace out of the rain. He never eats them up because I believe they taste awful. I wonder how we know this. Did some hero once eat one in the interests of science? One of the things I think I know is that somebody engaged in studying the causes of diabetes once took a sip of urine. It was very sugary, and bingo – the link was made. Sweet pee. Oh Lord. One has to admire these intrepid explorers into the realms of the unknown, especially those who take all the risks themselves. How differently one would feel about the manufacturers of cosmetics if they squirted chemicals into their own eyes instead of those of rabbits.

I am in misanthropic mood, having suffered an overdose of people, and at the moment I never want to see another one again. Janet sits in the parlour embroidering, the little girls play horrible music in the barns, the eldest son is ensconced in a remote corner with his new computer and I sit in the furthest room of the long house staring out of the window at the wet nettles and pondering the meaning of the

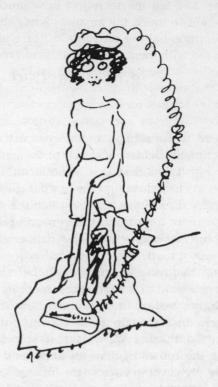

I have a vacuum cleaner
that came with attachments

universe. In order to do this more efficiently I have eschewed alcohol for the time being. So far this hasn't helped. I don't think I am programmed with the correct type of question.

The son (who is of a smugness intolerable since he has stopped smoking) says helpfully that if he had only brought a certain attachment for his computer he could have printed this for me. He has taken my mind off the meaning of the

universe, and led me to reflect how much I detest attachments – not so much the amatory kind, although in view of
the recent hoo-ha (the wedding of the Duke of York), I am
fairly bored with them too – but the kind that are intended to
be joined to some central master gadget. I have a vacuum
cleaner that came with attachments: things for sucking moths
out of the curtains, for delving down the sides of chairs after
stray coins, crumbs and crisps, for cleaning the stairs and
those little inaccessible corners; extra extension rods which
get very easily dented and refuse to join together; a little
hollow brush for dusting the surfaces; and the principal
attachment for cleaning the carpet. The last-named is
designed to flip over in order to clean the parquet and if you
lose control for a moment it flips over while you're cleaning
the carpet. The whole thing also gets easily choked, and at
this you have to fling it on its side, insert the nozzle
underneath, direct the tube out of the window, put it into
reverse and switch on – when it promptly blasts the obstruc-
tion into the garden. In theory. In practice you spend many
hours poking down it with an unwound metal coat-hanger.
All the attachments get mislaid, it loses its breath and its
power of suction and you're back to the dustpan and brush.

Worse, however – *much* worse – is a certain food processor
which has so many attachments that it really needs quarters
of its own. It has things for chopping and grating and
shredding, things for grinding and things for whipping. It
has a thing for taking the juice out of carrots and a thing for
kneading dough. It has all sorts of things that I don't know
the purpose of. It quite possibly has a thing for taking the
stones out of horses' hooves. But, most spectacular of all, it
has a thing for turning butter back into cream – which brings
us again to the meaning of the universe. It overturns all our
latest theories and conceptions; for turning butter back into
cream, like unscrambling eggs, is in direct contravention of
the second law of thermodynamics. I am rapidly coming

round to the view that all – all – is illusion and our world is most probably nothing but a bit of grit in the eye of some vast and indifferent Being. I expect I'll feel better when it stops raining.

Too many love songs

When I first listened to the wireless it really only had two programmes, known as Home and Light – described by my uncles as 'Home' and 'Away'. I still think of Radio 4 as 'Home' and Radio 2 as 'Light' and I never listen to Radios 1 or 3 because they both play the sort of music I don't like. I don't know which I hate more, the Rolling Stones or Mozart, although I expect I'm out of date and the Rolling Stones have rolled away by now. The daughter has tapes of the most horrible cacophony but I have no idea of who's making it. The extraordinary thing is that the beloved fourth son actually runs one of these groups and if I wasn't his mother but his father I would wonder if I was – if you follow me. Genetics is peculiar.

I usually listen to Radio 4, especially *The Archers* and anything that Brian Redhead says, but too often we are given what is known as 'another chance to hear . . .' which is BBC English for the same dish *réchauffé*. I seldom wish to hear a programme twice in one week except for *The Archers* and Brian Redhead, and for some reason *Down Your Way* – known round here as 'Up Yours' – drives me absolutely nuts, so every now and then I am compelled to listen to Radio 2.

Doing this the other morning as I washed the dishes I was struck by the fact that every single song was about love. For me, on a scale of one to ten, romance comes about eighth, after chess but before politics and football. I scarcely ever give it a thought. My mind is usually taken up with what to cook for lunch, or why I've got an overdraft when I've hardly bought anything, or where the daughter is, or who's going to feed the boa constrictor while its master is away on holiday, or why the mat from outside the bathroom is draped up the steps to the barn. Perhaps these topics are not suitable to be set to music, but surely somebody could think of something to sing about as well as love. The whole thing is entirely disproportionate. People go out to work or draw the dole, or take the clothes to the cleaners, or dine in Greek tavernas, or go to the races, or fill in tax forms, or wash their hair. All sorts of things they do before they start thinking about love. Except – and here I imagine is the crux of the matter – when brought low by Cupid's dart.

I have never met anybody who has been made as happy by love as he has been made sad. No one has ever danced for joy on my kitchen table, but many's the person who has lain her head on it and cried her little eyes out. No matter that the cause of the anguish is quite clearly – to the outside eye – a raving lunatic: usually sullen, often violent, some-times smelly. The smitten one is out of her mind (or his, as the case may be. We have learned recently that many women beat up their menfolk. Can this be true?) The smitten one wishes, out of her deep love, that either the loved one should devote every waking minute to her, or drop dead. They don't say that much in the songs they sing. I was talking recently, or rather I was mostly listening, to a friend whose love affair was not going well. 'It's over,' she said, wiping away a tear. 'Now all I want is that we should both emerge from it with our dignity intact.' It was already a bit late for that since she'd cut up his pyjamas with the kitchen scissors, but I listened sympathetically, nodding wisely every now and then. It didn't seem appropriate to point out that she was speaking untruthfully; that while she certainly wished to emerge with her dignity intact she didn't care if he came out backwards, screaming, with his hair on fire. They don't say that much either in the songs they sing.

I'm going to listen to the wireless now while I peel the spuds, and if it's *Gardeners' Question Time* I'm not going to turn to Radio 2, I'm going to turn it off. Then I'm going to compose a little song of my own, a Social Realist song about cat food and blocked drains; about the price of butter, and toenail clippings and rain. There are some quite nice songs about rain but they've all got love in them. Mine won't.

The egg and I

I have a tendency to go on about the extraordinariness of the egg. I think the meaning of the universe is bound up with the egg. In the exact spot I was gazing at the other day while wrestling with this problem, there was discovered a pheasant sitting on 18 of the things. This is called synchronicity. Unfortunately the mode of her discovery led to her precipitate departure. There was a baseball game in progress and the ball landed, wallop, more or less on top of her, whereupon she took herself off, leaving her clutch of orphaned, illegitimate eggs.

Next day we guiltily crept up to see whether she had come back and found that, while most of the eggs were cold, four of them were cheeping and their occupants were trying to make a break-out. At this we sent for the gamekeeper and asked for advice. He said the prognosis was not good, but helped the daughter and her friend extract the chicks. It is very odd to peel an egg and get not an egg but a damp, gawky baby. The gamekeeper shook his head dubiously but

the females of the party – and it seems that even the naughtiest female will move heaven and earth to keep an infant creature alive – rushed them indoors and set about constructing a premature baby unit. The gamekeeper had said they must be kept at 90 degrees, which presented a problem and a conflict of interests. Cadders has sequestered the airing-cupboard, which was the obvious place except that it has no light, which apparently is also necessary to the survival of chicks, and Cadders made it clear that not only would he eat them if he got the chance but he wasn't going to relinquish his place in the warmth.

Then I had one of those inspirations which are afforded to the chosen once or twice in a lifetime. Cat baskets are specifically designed not to let the cat out; ergo, by the same token, the cat can't get in. This is called lateral thinking, I think. The girls made up a bed of straw in a shallow casserole, arranged the chicks in it, stuck them in the cat basket and set it on the Aga. We had considered putting

them *in* the Aga, in the plate-warming oven, but I thought it much too risky. Roast pheasant.

Then one of the chicks died. The daughter, whose compassion is balanced by pragmatism, suggested giving it to Cadders since he obviously wanted one but I, who am totally unbalanced, forbade this. The remaining three are cheeping and kicking like anything. One of them presented some worry, refusing to open his beak to allow food in – the gamekeeper gave us some pheasant food which has to be squashed up and moistened with spit and offered on a stalk of grass, a wildly pernickety business – but by dint of perseverance even he is now sitting up and taking nourishment. Their feathers have dried and fluffed out and show their markings and they are awfully beautiful. I never thought I'd get fond of a pheasant because I always found them so thick, scuttling along the road in front of the car, while the whole of wild Wales beckoned, but these have crept into our hearts. It's early days yet and I'm fully prepared for them to die, but if they do it will be yet another sadness. I have tried to block from my mind the fact that if they live their fate is certain. Ghastly great oafs in silly socks will come along and shoot them. There is no skill involved in this. The pheasants round here are so tame and so dumb that a child could walk up to one and wring its neck with no trouble at all. I don't suppose I'll ever eat a pheasant again. It might be one of ours and I should feel like a sort of incestuous cannibal. We shall have to confine ourselves to bread sauce and game chips and redcurrant jelly and gravy made from a stock cube. I have a passionately vengeful fantasy of creeping up on the hunters and shooting them full of pellets.

I am fed up with the meaning of the universe. Everything starts in the egg and ends in death. I think it's called 'the heartbreak at the heart of things'. But then perhaps our very mortality is an egg and at the moment of death our souls will emerge like damp chicks. If this is so then everything is all right and I doubt there'll be any need for us to be dried off on top of the Aga. 'All things are well and all things will yet be well.' I think that's called optimism. Optimism is the last resort of those in deep despair. There can't be any optimists in heaven.

Fly in the ointment

High on the list of things a mother would prefer not to know comes the following.

'Hi, Mom.'

'Hullo, my darling, how are you?'

'I'm fine, Mom.'

'What have you been doing, darling?'

'Well, the other day I was going to take Crispin and his girlfriend up in an aeroplane. But before I could take passengers, according to regulations I had to take off and land once more. So the control tower said the weather was clear and I took off. Then I looked down and the San Fernando basin had disappeared under a blanket of cloud.'

'Good heavens, my darling.'

'So I radioed for instructions because I wasn't qualified to fly through clouds and they told me to fly to Ontario.'

'You flew to *Ontario*, my darling?'

'That's Ontario *California*, Mom.'

He had to spend the night in an hotel, and as far as I know Crispin and his girlfriend are still hanging about in the hangar. It was only 50 miles he had to go, but that's 50 miles flying through the air and I have frightfully little faith in aeroplanes. His younger brother set off in one the other day, and after the time specified for the trip I rang up to see if he'd arrived safely. Not a bit of it. His aeroplane had had to turn around in the middle of the Atlantic and come all the way back again. I don't know why. Metal fatigue? Engine failure? The pilot had forgotten his packed lunch? Ooh, I hate aeroplanes. I only ever went in one once and I didn't like it. The thing that scans you for concealed weapons at the airport screamed when I stood in it and a hostile-looking lady searched me. We think it was my earrings, but I don't place much faith in a gadget which is incapable of differentiating between a sub-machine gun and a bit of jewellery. Do I *look* like a terrorist?

The third son and his cousin were once flying across the Channel in an elastic-band-type aeroplane when the cousin, who was driving, was afflicted by a call of nature. The only receptacle handy was a 7-Up can, so the son took the controls while the cousin took time off. Then the slipstream took over and – but I can't bear to think about it.

Even here in the country we are not free of the aeroplane. The RAF practises low-flying – I think to escape radar – and weaving through mountain peaks, and the sound barrier cracks up all over the place. Cows drop their calves, sheep their lambs; and the chickens go off the lay. I would myself. As it is, I leap feet in the air and drop things. When the daughter was smaller she would jump the length of the kitchen from a standing start into the arms of the nearest person, howling with terror. It must have left its mark.

It is significant that the word airport has absolutely none of the glamour of the word seaport. When I hear the word seaport I smell tarry ropes and dead fish, I see vistas of swaying palms and hear breakers rolling, I remember sailors toiling at the shrouds (well, almost) and the controlled chaos of the docks. At the word airport I am assailed by a sense of boredom, an image of formica, carpet tiles and peculiar food in plastic trays. For some reason wafting away into the sky is not nearly as exciting as setting out to sea.

My friend Mary's friend Matthew ran out of money in Minorca and planned to spend the night at the airport there, but people came with brushes and mops to clean the lounge where he had arranged himself, and then they locked the place up so he had to leave and sleep under a prickly bush. He awoke to find a cat asleep on his chest and a cicada half in his mouth trying to climb down his throat. It wouldn't have happened in a seaport. He could have curled up on a coil of rope or climbed into a lifeboat or stretched himself out on his dunnage. In fact it would have been so interesting that he probably wouldn't have wanted to go to sleep at all.

In and out of the cage

The house is haunted by the echo of your last goodbye.
The place is cluttered up wi' roses that refuse to die
Di-dah-di-di-dah-didi-dah as it brings intimate
glimpses of intimate thi – ings

Fortunately that is all I can remember of that song. Gracie
Fields used to sing it but I don't think it ever really caught
on. You have to do it in a sort of mournful warbling
monotone and people don't like it much. It has been on my
mind because our younger children have whipped off to the
ends of the earth and we all feel rather odd. The older
children have been quite old for ages now, but the younger
two were mere infants until about five minutes ago when
one went to Los Angeles for his hols (fingers crossed that the
San Andreas fault hold together), and the baby went to
Africa for hers (fingers crossed for Lord knows what). I say
'baby' but she is actually now slightly bigger than me and I
have pinched a pair of her jeans to take on *my* hols. She is
also more sophisticated than me and much luckier, ringing
up to say goodbye from the VIP lounge at Gatwick before
boarding a plane owned, I believe, by her hosts.

I am writing this on the train to Glasgow, a nice enough
place I am sure but lacking the *je ne sais quoi* which I feel
Benin must possess. Never mind. I am free. It took me some
time fully to realize this. Caged animals suffer from the same
problem. Should somebody open the door, they carry on
sitting there listlessly, not understanding – in their dumb,

Tweet, tweet....

brutish fashion – that they can take off into the world. Me too. For a few days Janet and I drifted around the Welsh house wondering what had happened. No screams of 'I'm bored', no sorties to the shop for choc ices, no need to prepare huge teas, no mess, no piles of washing, no fun really. I have been hung around with kiddies like a tree with monkeys since my early twenties and Janet has had more than ten years of it. We have looked forward to this moment and now we don't like it. The doll's house and the air rifle and the little abandoned wellies all bring lumps to our throats and we can't remember quite what we're *for*. After a while of mooching glumly round in the rain (Janet says we don't have summer any more – just the rainy season) it slowly dawned on us that we could get up and go; whereupon we got up and went. Starting at 4.30 this morning.

I am wondering whether I shall now begin to be able to concentrate for more than ten minutes at a time, since for the larger part of my life I have felt that whatever I was doing, I should really be doing something else. Washing nappies I should have been painting pictures. Painting pictures I should have been mincing liver. Pushing the pram round the park I should have been hoovering the house, and hoovering the house I should have been doing it with a greater degree of thoroughness. I detested going out in the evenings, not only because I detest going out in the evenings, but because I was afraid I would return to find that the house had burned down and the children were gone. I was always quite surprised not to find the garden garnished with fire-fighting equipment and even now when I get home I still have to creep into the bedrooms to check that the occupants are present and breathing.

Not at the moment. The only helpless dependants at the moment are two cats and a boa constrictor, and Someone is coping beautifully with those, except that once he left the snake's door open; but the snake, whose thought processes are more sluggish than my own, simply lay in her cage until it banged shut again. Thinking about this, I have realized that there is a peculiar quality to my sense of liberty. It isn't so much that I feel free. I feel feral. This makes me sad, but as we can never return to a state of simple savagery I suppose I shall have to make the best of it. Anyway when the hols are over I shall be back inside.

what's for
supper, mum?

The restless earl

I was watching telly yesterday and wishing wistfully that I
could crawl into the set and throttle Brian Aherne, or at least
wring him out. He was portraying a writer of such wetness
that one felt one should be wearing one's mac. He had a son
who went to the bad and I don't blame him in the least. If I'd
been him I'd have started off with parricide and ended up
biting my nails. When it got too embarrassing I turned to
Ghost Stories of an Antiquary and when that got too frightening
I watched Brian Aherne again.

I was idling thus because until the daughter returns to school I regard this period as the hols. *My* hols. This is entirely irrational and I don't care. While I was doing this a small drama was enacting itself in the garden. Janet and the third son observed a strange couple out there and Janet enquired if she could assist them in any way.

'We are just lookink,' they said, 'because eet ees so beautiful.'

Flattered, the son said she should have asked them in to look round the home, but Janet took the view that it was kinder to leave them with their illusions intact. Admittedly they were foreigners, but we racked our brains for some time wondering what could so have taken their fancy. There's nothing in the garden at the moment but masses of leaves and one battered sweet pea. Perhaps they hie from a barren and leafless land.

Scotland was nice and green. I spent a day in Ayrshire with my friend Wendy and we went for a walk on a cliff top. The sun was shining and we were suddenly almost deafened by the sound of popping. Looking closely we saw the gorse pods bursting open. Now, Wendy and I were brought up in the same patch of Wales where you couldn't turn without falling over a gorse bush and neither of us had ever heard them pop before. In Arran I saw my first mink – on the hoof as it were, although I am also far from familiar with the coats made from his brethren – and I was surprised to find him a little ferrety creature. I think I had assumed they were built more on beaver lines. It must take millions of them to make a stole. Then I went for a ride on the back of a motor bicycle, and after that I went out on the sea in a titsy little boat to look in a lobster pot. To my intense amazement there was a lobster in it. We took him home to show everyone, but the consensus was that he was too young to leave his mother, so we put him back in the ocean. My host put his cat in the ocean too and got attacked by a couple of *Guardian* readers accusing him of cruelty. Actually the cat likes swimming and it would be mean to prevent him. Of course the couple had gone by the time we were being kind to the lobster.

Then we went to an evening of folk song and dance. Two wee girls hopped about a lot doing a highland reel and got an enormous round of applause, which led me to think it must have been cleverer than it looked; and then four more girls sang 'The Earl of Moray'. I am not, as I think I have said before, musical, but I happen to have a soft spot for ballads – they are so marvellously uncheerful – and I used to trill 'The Earl of Moray' under my breath day after day until I forgot about him. I had not given him a thought for years, but now I am undone. The blasted Earl of Moray is soonding thro' the toon every waking hour. He is driving me mad, that braw gallant. I don't even know what it's all about. Who was Huntley? Why wae – I mean woe – to him? Why did he slay the earl? What queen? What on earth was going on? It's like the vague village scandals I hear about whenever I go to the country. The locals assume you know the background and you leave it too late to ask, so you never find out the details. I have the same problem with the song 'The Queen's Marys'. Who got whom in the club? I know that any normal person with a proper education could answer my questions, but I also have a sneaky conviction that I was once told all about it anyway and I simply wasn't listening.

The Earl of Moray's back. His leddy is looking frae the castle doon. I wonder who *she* was and what she made of it all? I am humming under my breath. Oh please, God rest the Earl of Moray.

Man and machine

The other day I was shown a word processor in operation. The eldest son put some words of mine on it and I was astonished to see how authoritative they looked on the little screen. He put it through some of its tricks and I almost immediately became rather fond of it. It was so eager and obedient. 'Look,' said the son, 'I will tell it to find "Mary".' He twiddled something while I gazed enthralled, and a little arrow whizzed around like a terrier after a rat until it found Mary, whereupon it stood pointing and quivering with what looked like delighted triumph at its ability to please its master. How unlike people, I thought. How unlike children. How unlike the cats really, who live largely for themselves and are indifferent to the whereabouts of Mary.

I could imagine a bond springing up between machine and operator, similar to that between master and hound: the only drawback being that the word processor doesn't bark. The other night when I was away, the son was engrossed with his pet when Someone returned home to find the house locked and no lights on in the front. His knocking was not sufficient to distract the son, so he set about breaking in – not wishing to spend the night curled up in the geraniums. At the sound of breaking glass the son was alerted and promptly rang for the police who arrived with unusual alacrity and proposed to arrest the householder. Explanations followed with the householder apologizing for the misunderstanding and being assured by an indulgent policeman that he could do what he liked in his own house. Besides, the officer was pleased to have solved a crime.

This gave rise to interesting speculation. Say everyone in the Crescent was simultaneously struck by some virus and we all started breaking our windows. Would we be permitted to carry on without let or hindrance? This is rather reassuring if it is so. Now that we are barely permitted to smoke anywhere except on top of Snowdon I had thought all our liberties were being eroded and the heavy hand of the law would fall on the shoulder even of a chap smashing his own windows. Although it is, admittedly, still permissible to bash up your spouse – within limits – you have to be nearly (or completely) killed before you can turn in your loved one. I know a man who lives on an island whose wife went off to the mainland and returned with a brand-new hair-do. He didn't like it so he put the spaghetti bolognaise on it, and if I'd been her I'd have sent for the paratroopers. It is horrible to imagine combing strands of spaghetti out of your newly set hair: mince and tomato sauce and greasy bits of herb trickling into your eyes. It must have taken days of shampoo and rinsing before she stopped smelling like a trattoria.

Zélide knew a girl who was quietly sweeping up leaves, humming to herself and listening to the neighbours quarrelling when suddenly there came a silence. She carried on humming and sweeping for a while until the unaccustomed absence of yelling struck her as a bit sinister, so she peeped through the window. Picture the scene – the wife lying with the meat cleaver in her parting and the husband transfixed by the breadknife. Horror. They both spent some time in hospital and prison and then they decided to forgive and forget and move back in together: she – says Zélide – wearing a little woolly hat to hide the join and he in a cummerbund to keep him together. Now if we all eschewed the company of our fellows and got shacked up with a word processor none of this would ever happen. Would it?

Drawing the line

Two ancient sayings have run together in my mind: 'Don't you know there's a war on?' and 'Get in the queue.' 'Don't you know there's a queue on?' I mutter morosely to myself, and sometimes I wonder whether shopkeepers were barking these phrases at the public during the Wars of the Roses. They arise, I believe, from a peculiarly English cast of thought, and whether we always had this tendency to form ourselves into lines and permit ourselves to be verbally abused by those who are, theoretically, there to serve us is a question which I sometimes ponder in the watches of the night. I am feeling very bitter at present because I just had to queue to get myself shot full of typhoid and tetanus and cholera and goodness knows what else before I go to Egypt, and while it is bad enough having to queue to pay for your cornflakes, it is galling to have to queue to get yourself jabbed and made to feel ill. I remember when I was expecting the children and was supposed to trip regularly along to the hospital or surgery so that some doctor could take my blood pressure and listen to the foetal heart-beat. I wasted hours in hideous tedium before I decided it was all too much and if anything was wrong I would undoubtedly be the first to know about it and then I would go to the doctor. They were very hoity-toity and disapproving about this but I was past caring. Preventive medicine is undoubtedly a good idea and, I am sure, prolongs life, but if queuing up to get it renders a good deal of life maddeningly boring then it seems a bit pointless.

We were in the building society the other day. Eight places

for people to sit and transact business and only one in use. There was a bell on the counter labelled 'Enquiries' and after a while the man in front of us put his finger on it and kept it there. A disgruntled-looking person eventually emerged from the wings in answer, and the man in front of us said his enquiry was: why were there eight places for people to sit and transact business and only one in use? I admired him enormously for voicing this simple query which had been running silently in all our heads, and it worked. The disgruntled person actually sat down and did something. I think the man in front of us was a taxi-driver. There is something very competent and reassuring about taxi-drivers.

The bank is possibly even worse than the building society because you can *see* dozens of people wandering round behind the grille looking far from gainfully employed. They clutch sheaves of paper and look neither to left nor right – which we all know is a ruse to deceive the authorities. (I have heard of people who spent a lifetime walking the corridors of power clutching documents without ever doing a stroke of work.) The public stand meekly, except for one or two free spirits who mutter and shuffle and raise their eyes to heaven – and Janet. Janet once enlivened proceedings considerably by reading aloud a notice instructing us to wait there until a cashier position became available. What, she mused aloud, precisely *was* the cashier position? Did it differ materially from the missionary position? Was life in the bank perhaps more eventful than it appeared on the surface? Failing a Janet, perhaps we should all take to theft. If we are to believe what we see on telly, bank-robbers get in and out pretty smartish. Even breaking through into the vaults from the laundrette next door could well prove to be faster than queuing up.

October

Some progress

I am becoming extremely adventurous. Scotland yesterday, Egypt tomorrow. Perhaps I could turn into a foreign correspondent, although, having plodded the length of Camden High Street, I wonder whether travel is not somewhat redundant now that food from every obscure nook and cranny of the world is freely available within a stone's throw of the home. We had tempura from a Japanese-run stall for our lunch on Saturday, strolling round the souks of Camden Lock dribbling soy sauce down our fronts, and then Italian ice cream to follow – maple and walnut for me, tangerine and rum for my companion. I think I still feel a bit sick. It may have been the attempt to forget about my stomach where alien cultures – in, I dare say, several senses – were battling it out that put me into a philosophical frame of mind. Progress, I mused, is a peculiar concept.

When I got home I asked Someone where the notion of progress had arisen and he told me, but I've forgotten again. The snag in being married to a person who knows more or less everything is that one gets hopelessly lazy. (He of course says that he knows very little: it's just that I know absolutely nothing.) I never look things up in books because all I need to do is ask him, and when he gives me the answers I don't properly commit them to memory because I know if I forget all I have to do is to ask him again. It is rather like keeping one's brain in a suitcase.

I believe the chaps who originally formulated the idea of Progress considered it to be without question a thoroughly

Good Thing and I am far from in accord with them. I am glad that it has brought us Jif and Flash and Vim because the greasy rim on the bath does not submit to mere soap on the flannel; but looking at the stables which constitute a large part of the Camden Lock set-up and have progressed from housing horses to harbouring trestle tables of assorted junk, I felt nostalgic. I think some stupid bastard has ripped down a lot of the building, but I didn't investigate too closely because I didn't want to feel furious on top of feeling sick, and I suppose we should be grateful that so much has been retained even if it does have an air of rather contrived and tatty gaiety. The casual nature of the complex is imposed, and arises from nothing that was there before. The Greeks, I thought, grimly keeping my mind off ice-cream cornets, were *there* and we are *here*. There is no discernible link between us, and it cannot be claimed that what has happened in between is Progress – just a lot of time.

I had never previously deigned to visit this market because, if you live near something, you don't (I bet Parisians don't go up the Eiffel Tower), but my friend said he was going to buy Christmas presents and I was so impressed by this evidence of prudence and foresight that I went along to watch. I felt rather let down when we emerged with the strap from a Sam Browne belt, a rusty iron wheel that he found in a corner, and a riding-crop. He had intended buying every-body knives with things in them for taking stones out of horses' hooves but the man wasn't there. The riding-crop was adorned at the top with what looked like a wee hammer.

'What,' he speculated, 'is that for?'

'Well,' I said, 'it looks to me like a thing for banging things back into horses' hooves. Nails for instance. Idiot!'

I suppose it was success of a sort, and it is nice that trappings for horses are still available in their old home, but the smell of hot dogs and donner kebab and tandoori chicken

and peopole doesn't measure up to the smell of hay and horse manure.

Over-booked

'I believe we must spend the next five years finding ways of reallocating resources within the industry so that we market the product better overall and so that we strive to produce a

product which is going to be popular and of the highest quality. We have to do this together.'

When I started reading this (I confess I didn't get very far in the article) I thought it must be the voice of British Leyland or the National Coal Board, or perhaps the association of garden-gnome manufacturers; but no, it was somebody speaking for the dear old British book trade which is desperately seeking a place in the sun, or at any rate the high street. Apparently such concerns as Laura Ashley, Next and Benneton each have more than 200 'outlets', so they are in no danger of going down the communal drain. Marks & Spencer 'began as a small venture' and now are 'an important part of the high street'. Bookshops, on the other hand, are finding it harder and harder to pay high-street rents and are condemned, like unsuccessful abortionists, to the back streets.

The trouble is the *product*. In particular, there are *too many books*. M&S have succeeded in refining their product. One cucumber, as the poet says, is very like another and, more important, the cucumber is one of only a limited number of products on offer from St Michael to the housewife. Of books, on the other hand, as the Preacher said, there is no end: some 50,000 of the damn things appeared last year. If only these multiple titles could be reduced to, say, 100 standard lines – ideally to ONE BOOK written jointly by a committee of tried and tested best-selling authors: a work of 'faction' perhaps, incorporating the life story of Mary Queen of Scots, say, and the Rolling Stones, and the best parts of the Concise Oxford English Dictionary, illustrated by a few photographs of Edwardian country ladies and the latest royal wedding. It could be advertised, like any other product, on the telly. The book trade, like everybody else, would be rich and happy.

Better still, we could do without the *authors* altogether. 'One characteristic that I envy of all those companies is that they don't negotiate terms; they don't take somebody else's output and decide which part of it they want to buy. They identify their customers' needs and then manufacture quantities and qualities which they can sell at a price which customers can afford . . . As their success grows they are able to pay levels of rates and rents that an operation like ours cannot match.' The idea is not foolish. What indeed is the point of all these books, if we discount the vanity of authors? Judging from the publishers' blurbs, most of them are duplicates – literary cucumbers, so to speak, with as little nutritive value but very much more expensive.

I asked Someone for his view on the matter, since publishing is the vineyard in which he toils (and increasingly spins). He says that educated people buy very few new books. They just read the reviews. Reviews don't sell books: indeed the opposite, since they tell you what you want to know in a book while saving you the fag of ploughing through the attendant verbiage. But fortunately there are very few educated people around these days.

Certainly this house, I reflect, is a monument to the book trade, or at any rate the book trade of yore. Someone has distributed his 10,000 dusty tomes in three separate rooms –

the scholar's library containing dictionaries and so on, and texts in unknown languages; the gentleman's library with books 'which any sensible man would want to read and reread' such as *The Decline and Fall of the Roman Empire*; and the ladies' library with books 'which you admire for their outsides'. All are arranged by colour, which not only furnishes a room, he says, but maximizes the uniformity of the product.

Holiday reading

Cairo

Before setting out on the hols I grabbed a few books more or less at random, except that I imposed on myself a certain discipline, eschewing the Agatha Christies, Margery Allinghams, Patricia Wentworths, Ngaio Marshes etc that I usually take for relaxation. There is absolutely nobody who writes like them any more, so it is fortunate that I always forget who dunnit and can re-read them constantly. This time I took Rose Macaulay's *Orphan Island* (not her best), *Madame Bovary*, some Maupassant short stories and Hugh Lloyd-Jones's translation of the *Oresteia*. They weren't enough, of course, so I had to read them all twice – and a guide book to Alexandria and two four-day-old *Telegraphs*. From one of these I learned that a book teaching the kiddies how to live with daddy when he emerges from the closet and shacks up with his friend had been circulating in London schools, and reflected that I only have to turn my back on the country for five minutes and it goes mad. I seem to remember a picture of two chaps with no pyjamas sitting up in bed smiling, with a puzzled-looking child between them. They are taking

123

breakfast. As I wrote that, the thought occurred to me that perhaps I had got a touch of the sun and had been hallucinating, so I looked up the newspaper in question and there it was: *Jenny Lives with Eric and Martin*. There is a packet on the breakfast-tray with something Knacke written on it. Is this a joke? What is a joke? It has quite ruined my holidays, since half the fun of being abroad is observing the strange ways of foreigners and I do assure you that there is nothing here to compare in sheer nuttiness with that book. There is no satisfaction in remarking, 'Well, of course things are quite different in England,' if the difference lies in the fact that the English are getting rapidly weirder. Sometimes when I go out I go 'covered' in order to look less conspicuous and Ingleesy. I have acquired a wee hat and a thing to drape round it and am mostly taken for Turkish.

I have also acquired a pile of brightly coloured mats and two donkey panniers to carry them in. Not to mention a bird-cage and a walking stick. We were negotiating for a cat-basket but luckily the price went through the roof. I say 'luckily' because it is the third son who will have to carry most of these things and I inadvertently mentioned the cat-basket while we were sitting over a bottle of 7-Up. There was a rather terrible silence. When he had gained sufficient control he asked – very quietly, '*What* cat basket?' It was clearly the final straw and he would have denied all knowledge of me at the airport. We were sitting outside a café one evening when an itinerant salesman tried to sell us a chrome hat-stand. 'Stop me,' as the son observed, 'and buy one.' However, I do know where to draw the line.

Relaxing over *Madame Bovary*, I was surprised to find that I had previously misunderstood this book. I had read it first as an innocent girl and had failed to notice that her love affairs were not all in the mind, assuming that the poor lady lived in frustrated fantasy. When I discovered what she had been up to she lost my sympathy. It seems to me she had a most eventful time – not the years of undiluted provincial tedium I had thought were her lot. I got exasperated when everything ended with the mouthful of arsenic. Agatha Christie would have *started* there. As it was, no questions seem to have been asked at all and the ending is highly unsatisfactory.

The other book I have been studying is an English-Arabic phrase book. I haven't got very far and am feeling stupid. I sound stupid too. If all you can say is 'Please' and 'Thank you', 'The moon is beautiful' and 'A mosquito has bitten me on the stomach' then you're not going to sound like Brain of Britain. Happily most of the people I meet can speak some English and are charmingly patient and polite. In response I smile a lot and have hidden the *Daily Telegraph* in case anyone should glance through it. With the language problem I can't see how I would ever be able to explain that one away. I have already had some trouble trying to persuade a gentleman that he was wrong in supposing that the majority of English mothers habitually sell their daughters into prostitution and live off the proceeds. We are a very respectable people, I told him – very sane, very sensible and we look after our daughters most carefully. But that was before I'd seen Jenny breakfasting in bed with Eric and Martin.

Phrase and fable

Phrase books seem to be a universal and eternal source of hilarity and I think I know why. Their authors go mad in the course of compiling them. If you know how to do something – for instance speak your own language – you can go crazy trying to put across the basics to a load of idiots. I once wrote a book about how to feed babies – how long to boil their wee eggs for them, etc – and time and again I found myself addressing my imagined reader in tones of impatience and hostility: 'Oh go and ask your mother how not to burn water, you silly thing.' I had grown to picture my reader as dreadfully unhygienic and monumentally stupid, forgetting that I myself had once not known the rules about poaching and boiling and roasting and had in my time done some jolly weird things to some perfectly good food.

This, however, is beside the point. What I was saying was in connection with the phrase book I bought in order to bone up on my Arabic. The author's preoccupations, prejudices and thought processes are perfectly fascinating. Opening the book at random one finds the useful phrase: 'My friend whom you saw the other day died last night.' This is followed by the logical 'What happened to him?' To which the answer comes: 'A drunken soldier killed him in front of my house.' Then, I think, the author went off for a glass of mint tea, because he changes tack and goes into millinery: 'Whose hat is this?' Is she willing to sell it?', and then back to more significant matters: 'She was groping in the darkness.' 'I wish to live and die with you.' There is quite a lot of sex and violence here as you riffle through. 'He advised me not to take her by force.' 'I hit him because he did not tell the truth.' 'If he does this another time I shall beat him.' 'He has torn my clothes and spoilt my work. Please prevent him (from) doing this again.'

I personally found Alexandria not quiet (every vehicle has at least two horns in case one conks out) but remarkably pacific and unthreatening. We roamed round the streets and up and down the Corniche in the middle of the night and so, apparently, did everybody else, all good-naturedly sucking sugar cane or eating roasted corn cobs, or mango ices. I wouldn't idle round Camden Town in the middle of the night, I can tell you; so I don't know why my phrase-book man is so paranoid. He's nervous about health too: 'I feel pain in my tummy when I touch it.' 'It is nothing.' 'I think you are wrong.'

Some lines further on we have the reassuring 'Help yourself to a piece of bread and butter,' and 'Good people go to Heaven when they die.' I can't really imagine having occasion to make that last remark. Would one utter it in a reflective fashion, as though it had just occurred to one, or does it conceal a veiled threat? It is preceded by 'She cannot cross the street alone,' which certainly applies to me. Substitute 'I' for 'She' and I was yelling that phrase every time we left the house. Crossing the road in Egypt is like trying to cross the M1 and thoughts of death were constantly on my mind. We are also offered 'You must drive in the middle of the street,' and I can't figure that one out. Everyone drives in the middle of everything and there aren't any rules at all. How about: 'She was wearing her new hat and riding her old car.' 'Never mind.' Can anyone follow the sequence of thought there?

The following is simpler: 'What is the colour of your horse?' 'It is white.' 'Give me a small bottle of red ink.' You can see the madness beginning to take hold. The author is going to throw red ink all over that boring old horse. He's going to be rude to the cook too: 'Who is this ugly woman?' 'She is our cook.' 'I cannot look at her face.' He really hates the cook. 'The cook has burnt the cooking.' 'A fly has fell [sic] in my coffee.' This last sentence is of course indispensable if you want to make jokes, only I can't find the Arabic for 'Waiter, waiter!' or 'Soup'.

I keep getting side-tracked. I am now utterly riveted by the end of page 15: 'Do you like it on the first or second floor?' 'We have a big one in the upper storey.' 'We like to have one downstairs.' 'What happened to your trousers?' I think I can follow his train of thought here only perhaps I'd better not.

'Arabic phrasebook: "What
happened to your trousers?"'

He is ostensibly speaking of bedrooms which is tricky to start with. Let us leave him in his more philosophic vein: 'We can often (many times; frequently) dispel (drive away) gloom (grief; sorrow) by laughter (or laughing).' How very true.

November

Universal aunties

While I was in Egypt I was offered a dish with the words 'If you're Welsh you're going to enjoy this.' 'This' was a glutinous green soup and it was indeed delicious, but I would have found it perfectly agreeable if I'd been Abyssinian, and I cannot imagine where the mysterious Welsh connection comes in. That was not the only time these words were spoken to me. On several occasions I was offered some arcane delicacy with the assurance that my Welshness would cause me to find it palatable. I didn't like to disappoint the kindly cooks so I never denied the assumption, but I did puzzle over it. Did those tribes who were streaming all over the place and getting themelves lost at various moments in history, at some point cross tracks somewhere between Gizeh and Pen-y-Bont Fawr?

While I didn't actually understand any Arabic I could pronounce it very well because it has sounds remarkably similar to the Welsh 'll' and 'ch' – two sorts of cough you produce from the back of your throat and the back of your teeth. My Welsh comprehension isn't too good either, but I can make the right noises, and I wonder whether the scholars haven't somehow failed us in not making the connection between these two interesting and vital peoples. Once started I couldn't stop thinking along these lines.

Religion? Well, at a push, Islam isn't all that dissimilar to low-church Protestantism, and I met several people who visited the mosques with the frequency with which the Welsh used to go to chapel. Dress? We can't claim much present

'If you're Welsh you're going
to enjoy this..'

similarity here, but our local Welsh saint – one Melangell – certainly wore the same sort of headdress still seen in Egypt. (Yes, I know everyone did in the middle ages. Shut up. You're spoiling my theory.) Temperament? Hmmm. Both are to some extent an odd mixture of insularity and inquisitiveness, but so are lots of other people. Both have a strong sense of family – of extended family – and here I think we have real evidence of a link.

The Egyptians and the Welsh have more aunties than anyone else in the world. Wales is crammed with aunties, and so are Cairo and Alexandria and Port Said. I met dozens of aunties in these places and sipped tea and Coca-Cola with them. Some of them are also mothers, but this is somehow of less significance than their auntie-hood. Perhaps because one can have only a limited number of children oneself, whereas if one has enough brothers and sisters there is almost no limit to the amount of people who may call one 'Aunt'. Once established as an aunt, actual consanguinity ceases to matter and people who are entirely unrelated to you will refer to you by this title followed by your Christian name. (I should myself find this absolutely maddening, which leads me to suspect the validity of my own Welsh origins. They can't go very far back.) My own aunts – all nine of them – have died, so perhaps this is why I find other people's aunts so reassuring.

Two entirely strange Alexandrian ones were sitting on a café balcony, gazing out over the sea where the third son was disporting himself while I sat nearby in the shade reading Flaubert (in English: my French is lousy too) when suddenly they began to exhibit signs of anxiety. They turned to me with expressions of alarm and concern clearly occasioned by the apparent disappearance of the lad. My heart stopped. The third son, I thought to myself, has just gone down for the third time and the aunties don't know how to tell me. I went whiter than white and started to shake –

132

although I must admit I have a tendency to panic if anyone is five minutes late home. The aunties took my hands and made sounds of consolation and reassurance, whereupon the son emerged from the foam greatly exasperated by the fuss and protesting that he had been in no danger at all. The aunties and I, however, knew better. We continued to jabber at each other, this time in relief and gratitude and rage at men in general for the worry they cause us. We each knew perfectly well what the others meant, and as I left one of them followed and kissed me on both cheeks. And whether or not our races are related I shall love that auntie until the day I die.

Facing facts

The daughter's karate teacher at her convent school has instructed her that if she is attacked in the street she must throw her assailant to the ground and then, suppressing any maidenly misgivings, she must feel absolutely no compunction whatsoever in jumping up and down on his face. When I was a little girl I was specifically discouraged from jumping up and down on people's faces. I once bit a playmate in the leg because he was trying to push me into a gorse bush. He told his mother and she was furious with me. I have slapped faces occasionally because in my youth you couldn't see a film that didn't show some hero having his face slapped if he stepped out of line, but then rape wasn't really in style. Perhaps now that it is so prevalent men expect to have their faces leapt on. The daughter seems to take it all for granted and I am deeply alarmed at the rise in the level of violence. Admittedly on Saturday I watched Bette Davis going a bit further than face-slapping. She shot Claude Rains, but that was because he was threatening to tell her husband that he had been more to her than a music teacher. Nowadays, of course, Paul Henreid (the aforementioned husband) would be very much astonished if that hadn't been the case, it being widely assumed that no man and woman can spend more than five minutes alone without gaining carnal knowledge of each other. (Come to think of it that has always been the assumption, only chaperones prevented it from happening.) Violence too has always been with us. Once upon a time no one could open a cupboard in a film without a body falling out. You only had to see a cupboard to know that it concealed a body, but it never really caught on outside the silver screen. Not like face-slapping.

I was grumbling about the state of the world to Someone only this morning and he remarked that he had been thinking for some time about how strange it was that people were now yearning nostalgically for 'conventional weapons'. After the First World War everyone went off the idea – it was to be the war to end all wars – and now that we are faced with the threat of universal extinction by a mere spot of button-pushing, there is a wistful feeling that it would be nice to go back to the old sort: those dear little tanks and trenches and mortars and things.

On Sunday I watched Charlton Heston playing a person known variously as El Syd and El Seed having a terrible time trying to cope with a lot of intransigent Spaniards and Moors while keeping his honour unsullied. (I was irresistibly reminded of a comprehensive school headmaster. The task is impossible, but one is torn between a rather condescending pity and breathless admiration.) What was noteworthy was the extreme roughness of war, and I was forced to realize that nothing would persuade me to get on a horse and gallop into a group of enemies with the option of killing or being killed, not to mention having an arm or a leg chopped off in the mêlée. It all looked horribly dangerous, sweaty and unhealthily intimate, and speaking as a female I could see the attraction of sitting in a nice clean bunker with a polystyrene cup of instant coffee beside one, a button to push and not a single hostile face in sight. Men have never been as averse as women to the idea of hand-to-hand combat, but they only constitute half the human race. In *El Cid* Sophia Loren wasn't jumping up and down on anyone's face. Her nice clean frocks and hats made a pleasant contrast to all the bloodstained chain-mail, and while I accept that our daughters must learn somehow to protect themselves, and might have to dirty their clothes, it does seem an awful pity. I would myself murder with my bare hands anyone offering harm to my daughter, but I wish the necessity were not so likely to arise, and I am annoyed at the inconsistency thus revealed in my attitude.

Winter blues

I am suffering from one of those periodic bouts of tedium vitae. I think it began a few days ago when one of my friends asked eagerly what we were doing for Christmas this year. I haven't even finished with last Christmas yet – the little frocks I bought for my god-daughter and her baby sister are still sitting (for some reason) in the china pantry. It may sound far-fetched, but every single day since last December I have told myself that tomorrow I will post them off. Now of course it's too late because the little frocks will be much too little. I should have bought them shares in British Telecom or copies of *War and Peace* or something. Clothes are always a mistake.

Then yesterday Someone decided it was time we caught up on what the knickers-and-vicars press was up to these days, so he went out and bought all the Sunday tabloids and we sat glued to them and didn't have lunch until 3 o'clock. By that time I didn't much fancy lunch. I haven't been so swiftly depressed since I read *Oblomov*. What with murders and child abuse and Aids and rumours of war I felt quite nostalgic for the days when all I worried about was the Bomb. The head rings with the thud of apocalyptic hoof beats, and the heart is not raised by stories of blisteringly boring pop stars and soap stars – their figures (some have got too fat and some are getting too thin) and their families (some are getting married, some are getting divorced and some have lost their relations). Goodness, how one does not care. Forests have died to bring us these tidings and birds have lost their homes. I am getting to the point of depression where the sight of a lost worm will cause me to burst into tears.

The time has also come to turn on the central heating and I am of a generation which mistrusts central heating, suspecting it of causing dry rot in the home and bronchitis in the person. It mostly doesn't work properly either, and it costs a fortune. I don't like the idea of water circulating round the house. Sooner or later it's going to get out – it did in the country and we haven't even got central heating there. Some little pipe split in the frost and drowned the books and we are about to travel down with the express purpose of preventing this from happening again. Not, perhaps you will agree, the most cheery motivation for a trip. We have to turn off the water at several sources and I don't know where they are. It all starts half-way up a vertical mountain but I don't know where the hell it goes after that. I hope Janet does, because if we can't find the salient points it will end up in the bookshelves again.

Oh, it is winter in my soul and my woollen socks have

been consumed by the moth. I have left my windproof leather jacket in somebody's house and I can't be bothered to go and get it. I have no sensible shoes and my boots are down at heel. The cats too are aware of the coming of the cold. Puss askes to go out and then when I open the door she looks at the weather conditions and refuses to go further. I am always intrigued by the question of what her intentions might be then because, even if you're a cat, when you've got to go you've got to go.

I was sobbing away like this last night to my dear Caroline and she said she had just received a message from a friend, relaying some words of Mrs Thatcher to the effect that the Cenotaph 'brought hope and comfort to all our citizens'. Her friend said he liked that '*all* our citizens' because that means each and every one of us and he'd often wondered what kept, for instance, Francis Bacon going in his vale of tears, and now he knew. It's the Cenotaph. Caroline and I have agreed that if things get any worse we are going together to visit this monument and cheer ourselves up – if, that is, we can find our winter coats.

Organizing Alfred

One of the advantages of having grown-up children is that they tend to listen to you and take note of your tantrums. The eldest son rolled up in the country with some friend the other morning – circa 3 o'clock – and proceeded to make tea and toast and animated conversation immediately below my bedroom. I woke with a start, flew out of bed and screamed a few words down the stairs. They were instantly silent which would not have been the case some years ago. Some years ago they would have been silent for a moment; then there would have been whispers and giggles, growing quite rapidly into another crescendo, and I should have been up all night, roaring at them. These charming and responsible adults quietly gulped their tea and crept off to sleep in the barns.

Alfred came with us to Wales on this last trip and I was reminded of the time when the children persuaded him to go down through the trap door and make clandestine Marmite sandwiches in the middle of the night. The plot was that he should pass them up and then the children would haul him up too, but they went back to sleep. I didn't know about it at the time. Alfred only told me recently. He said he stood under the trap door for hours freezing cold, trying to shout under his breath – much too frightened to climb up the creaky stairs in case he wakened me. I must have been the most frightful ogress and poor Alfred was possibly the only thoughtful and responsible child that God ever created. I must remember to make it up to him one day.

Then there was the time we were having trouble with the boiler. It wouldn't boil by day, but each night it became a burning, fiery furnace and heated the water to the point where it threatened to blow the lid off the cistern and the roof off the cottage. I explained to Alfred that if he heard the water seething and surging, he must go into the bathroom and turn on all the taps. So he did that. Only I'd heard it too and came along, clad in a white nightdress and carrying a candle, enveloped in clouds of steam. The wretched boy nearly died of fright. He's still frightened of ghosts, sensing the blinking things everywhere, and such fear is contagious. Now I know that half-seen presences have been chasing Alfred I refuse to go alone to the wood pile in the evening. I make Alfred go.

Janet is only really frightened of spiders and we had a confrontation with one of them on Friday. For some reason there was a pile of socks on the dining-room windowsill; so I picked them up, muttering that they were covered in cobwebs. As I spoke, the author of the cobwebs stirred amongst them, and I must confess that we all screamed, me flinging the socks back on to the window-sill where, as far as I'm concerned, they can fester all winter.

'Oh God,' moaned Janet, shuddering, 'you know what it's doing in these socks, don't you? It knows it's getting cold and it's going to wear one on each leg.'

The purpose of our trip was to turn off the water so it wouldn't burst the pipes again, but by some horrid irony the water turned itself off. Its source got clogged up with mountain debris and Alfred had to climb up the stream to clear it. Then with the arrival of the son we realized that we would have to leave the turning-off operation to him because we could hardly abandon him and his friends to a waterless cottage. A totally pointless exercise in fact, although the countryside was beautiful, almost leafless and exposed. The most maddening thing is that I missed Jeff's party. I bet they didn't have any trouble with the water there.

Body search

The daughter and I and her friend Anna went off to the British Museum on Saturday to look at Pete Marsh, only we couldn't find him. We couldn't find Old Ginger either. I kept approaching officials intending to learn where these dead people had been positioned and then refraining out of some obscure sense of delicacy. It seemed too ghoulish to go flying around simply looking for bodies. Last time I was in a museum was in Cairo, and a guide with a gun slung over his shoulder (there were big notices everywhere forbidding the public to address one single word to these guides, so I guess their function was other than to direct one to Tutankhamun) beckoned us aside, and whispered that if we crept round the back of a certain sarcophagus we would be able to see the body because the outer casing had a hole in it. So we did and we couldn't. As far as we could tell there wasn't anything in there at all. We were rather disappointed.

Our little party then got distracted by the Assyrians and their winged monsters and fruitless speculation as to what it must have been like living in those times. A bit alarming I should imagine, although I don't suppose they had to fill in as many forms as we do. Of course I shouldn't like to be in a fold with the Assyrians coming down like a wolf on it, but I sometimes think death might be preferable to coping with the reams of paperwork of which so much of our present existence seems to consist. If our government scribes had to chisel out their silly and impertinent questions on basalt I bet that would serve as a disinducement to them.

I put aside these bitter reflections when we came to a colossal pot in a glass case. I have a passion for enormous earthenware containers but this one was really over the top. What could its purpose be, I wondered? It was certainly not intended to hold a bunch of flowers. When in doubt, I told myself, read the instructions. With me this involves donning the spectacles and then remembering to take them off before venturing a further step, because if I attempt to walk while wearing them I always fall over, which embarrasses the children. The author of the instructions was none too clear about the function of the pot either. He thought it must have been made in sections because it was huge, and he thought it might have been intended as a storage jar for grain or olive oil, and he thought that, in the end, it might have been used to put dead people in. I removed the spectacles and stood back to consider this proposition. The jar has a very narrow top and I couldn't think how they would have got their grain or olive oil out of it. It would have taken at least four strong men to tip it up when the time came to make a little vinaigrette or whatever, and I could not begin to think how they would have got a body in it. All chopped up in weensy bits? Ugh. And when bodies are cremated they require no larger container than a cocoa tin so the whole thing was most confusing.

We then moved on until we came to another pottery container.

'That,' I said in a psychic flash, 'is a bath. And I bet you anything you like they used to bury bodies in it too.'

The daughter protested that it was too small to be a bath, and I said it was a sitz-bath.

Slapping the specs back in place I stepped closer to peruse the card, and I was absolutely right. I really can't think how I came so quickly to the correct conclusion, because after all it would not occur to us nowadays to bury our loved ones in the bath – or stuff them in the cruet, come to that. The past is very, very peculiar, or else the interpreters of it have got it a bit wrong. We will never exactly know and I find it frustrating. Next time I'm going straight to Pete Marsh, who can't be any more of a *memento mori* than the rest of the museum, or perhaps we'll take a picnic to the cemetery and at least get some fresh air while we ponder the Last Enemy.

December

Sea fever

I have always had a soft spot for boats. My grandpapa was a sea captain until he came ashore and bought himself a pub, and my papa would have gone to sea if my grandpapa hadn't shot himself. I don't know why this sad event should have circumvented my father's ocean-going career, but it did. As it was, the house was crammed with books about boats, and sea yarns about monsters of the deep, and ghost ships, and mysterious happenings in lighthouses – all pertaining to the days of sail when life was more colourful. I can't summon up much romantic enthusiasm for tankers and nuclear subs or hydrofoils. I would have gone to sea myself if I had been born a boy, although perhaps it's just as well I wasn't since I can't tell my left from my right unless I visualize holding a knife and fork, and I can never remember which is port and which is starboard and which red and which green. My friend P. devised a mnemonic to help me but by the time I'd remembered how to work it out I'd have had the boat up a lamp-post. I can't remember what to say when the boom swings round either. 'Duck, you fool' is not the correct terminology. I sublimated all my oceanic yearnings when I was a girl by choosing sailors as my closest friends. There were hundreds of cadets around in those days, the training ship *Conway* providing a plentiful local source.

P. and his brother have gone boat mad and spend all their spare time taking lessons from Eric the sailor. He tried to teach me something about the names of bits of boats and I've mastered the poop deck and the main deck and the fo'c'sle

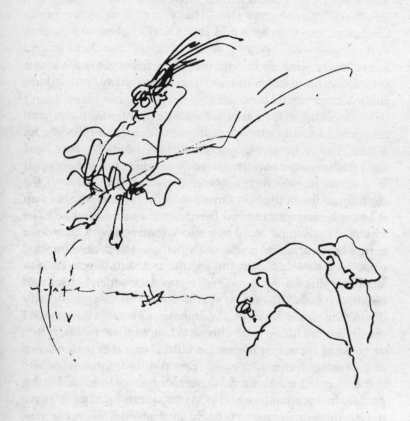

'Thar she blows'

and the fore mast and the main mast and the mizzen mast, and I know which is the sharp and which the blunt end, but learning the names of ropes is something like learning Russian, with warps and sheets and springs and halyards and topping lifts and running backstays and shrouds, and goodness knows what else. The parts of sails are pretty confusing too, with luffs and cleats and leaches and roaches and cringles – oh, bother it. I had a vague idea that living in a boat might simplify things. If the home life got too onerous one could up anchor and sail the home away, but I don't think that any more.

We went off to look at boats for sale (sale!) at the weekend and when I finally get sick of the house, I think I'll settle for a tent. I may have taken a more than normally jaundiced view of the matter because we were ambling round boatyards in a Force 10 gale with horizontal rain cutting through the clothing to the bone, and I'm never at my best when the hair is being blown off my head by roaring south-westerlies. The vision of flopping around in a sun-kissed sea with the waves gently lapping seems particularly remote when the aforesaid waves are breaking over the lighthouse. Nor is one encouraged by phrases such as 'Well, you'd better get that fixed because you don't want to spend your time hanging upside down with your head in the bilges.' Certainly not. I don't much like the idea of the chemical toilet in the heads either, or cooking *coq au vin* over a paraffin flame. Eric can do that and I admire him enormously. Eric is a traditional sailor and can do almost anything from welding steel to mending his pants. He's pragmatic too. He says it doesn't matter so much if you make an ass of yourself tossing around out on the briny, but when you sail the boat home you want to park (no, tie her up) properly because in all likelihood a lot of wiseacres will be lining the shore, pointing and giggling.

I think until the weather calms down I shall give up all idea of going down to the seas again in a tall ship – or a short ship, come to that. I shall sit by the fire and read a book about the *Cutty Sark*, keeping the powder (and the mascara) dry.

Pack drill

Janet went off and bought us a new duvet recently because the feathers in the old one had migrated into one corner, which just about served to keep Someone's feet warm. I have no quarrel with the new duvet, but I'm terribly bored with the cardboard box it came in. It is still sitting in a corner of the bedroom doing nothing for the elegance of this already overcrowded chamber. I hate cardboard boxes. In the country all our shopping comes packed in cardboard boxes and they pile up in no time, together with milk bottles and egg cartons. Someone has evolved quite a good method of dealing with them. He leaves them out in the rain, so they go all limp, and then jumps on them. This is effective, but I find it somehow unseemly and cannot bring myself to do likewise. It seems rather amateurish and makeshift. I would prefer to disassemble them so that they go flat, only I can never wrench the staples out. In order to burn them you have to tear them to bits, and then you have to keep relighting them because the bits lie on top of each other, like the pastry in cream slices, and the flames can't get a hold. They are maddening things and only cats love them. Quite often I go to pick up a cardboard box and a cat leaps out, inducing incipient cardiac arrest. Why, I asked Janet, did they have to pack duvets in cardboard boxes anyway? Ours was also already sealed in a stout plastic bag, which I would have thought quite adequate to exclude dust and moth. She explained that it would be difficult to keep piles of unboxed duvets in the shop because they would slither about and topple over, but I'm not convinced.

Manufacturers are potty about packaging. I'm sure they give it more thought than the stuff inside. I have broken my fingernails on biscuit packets and practically pulled out teeth on frozen food bags – the scissors are always missing when it's time to heat up the peas. Those childproof medicine bottles are proof against anyone but children, whose ingenious little minds are currently conversant with puzzles. Most people forget how to do puzzles when they reach maturity. I can see why eggs and meringues and squashy chocs have to be put in rigid boxes, but why do tights and stockings have to come armoured in the ubiquitous cardboard? Even ciggies have three layers of protection, which seems excessive, and toothbrushes and the better class of pen come in virtually impregnable containers. I used to get cross when tubes of toothpaste came in additional cardboard boxes – I expect the reasoning behind this is that, unboxed, they would slither about and topple over – but I prefer tubes to the new missile-type container. Shaving foam comes in precisely similar missiles and it is very horrible cleaning one's teeth with shaving foam. It can't be too pleasant shaving with toothpaste either.

Everything is wrapped up and I remember wistfully the days when I had to scrape the grocer's grubby thumbprints off the cheddar. The cheddar now may be frightfully hygienic but its consistency is peculiar. I had a fierce battle with two hamburgers last night – plastic tray, madly gripping clingfilm and cardboard box, all popped in yet another plastic bag.

When I was in Egypt I noticed very little packaging. On our arrival Abdul, the porter, went and bought us some falafal off the street in an old copy of *Al Ahram*. The meat

'In Egypt I noticed very little packaging...... but Egyptian ladies
are all wrapped up yours aren't.'

hangs on hooks in the open air with its tail still on, and little boys chase the flies off the bread with a whisk.

Now I've got a theory about this. In Egypt chastity is of supreme importance and here it isn't. Egyptian ladies are all wrapped up, and ours – weather permitting – aren't. Nevertheless all people have their quotient of puritanism and ours has simply taken on another form. It has put everything except people into chastity belts, and it will be interesting to see what happens now that Aids threatens to curtail all the jolly freedoms. For the first time in years I have read articles boldly extolling the values of chastity and fidelity – not many as yet, but the tide is beginning to turn. The moment I find myself able to buy dirty cheese and loaves with a sprinkling of fag ash I shall know that morality has returned to its proper sphere and I won't have to worry any more about breaking my fingernails on cardboard boxes.

Patronizing patterns

Sometimes life seems so short it's barely worth putting one's name in the telephone book and other times it seems to be going on for ever – drearily. When it's being fun it never looks as though it's going on for ever. The approach of the festive season is an odd mix of both. I can't decide whether I wish it would come quickly so we could get it over with, or slowly so that I can get ready for it. Or whether the simplest move is just to cut one's throat at the beginning of Advent and forget the whole thing. I can't even buy whisky now without it being in a cardboard box so it looks like a 'gift': a golden cardboard box with a semblance of red ribbon painted on it. Grrr. The bin-liner is bulging with these wretched boxes, when really whisky should come in medicine bottles on the Health Service, since one only takes it to retain one's sanity in the face of the turkey and the mistletoe. I started snivelling in church last night and sneaked out before some kind person could ask me what was wrong. Church seems a most inappropriate place to confess that one is sobbing because Christmas is coming.

I was also irritated by the new designer paving-stones to which the council has treated us and which go along Arlington Road past my place of worship. There is nothing really all that wrong with these non-slip stones except that I don't think they're stone at all and they're very small and some of them are *very* small – brick-sized – and every now and then somebody has waxed artistic with them and popped some of the very small ones in amongst the small ones, making a pattern. I wouldn't mind if the stone-layer had done it by himself in a fit of *joie de vivre*, or to ease the tedium, but these patterns have the air of being designed by a distant offical who learned at architectural school that the brute populace needs a little variety in its surroundings in order to keep it meek and well-behaved. They are horribly patronizing patterns and make me think dismally of shopping precincts. They have the same effect on me that hats have. People in hats look fearfully self-consciously pleased with themselves and one longs to tip their silly hats over their silly faces. (Just think of Peter Wright.)

There is a sinister rumour too that our council are going to be kind to us in the matter of our street market. That is, they might move it altogether into some covered area where everything will be much nicer and more hygienic. Certainly a lot of tidying up has been going on and new supermarkets are proliferating all over the place. There is a heated argument in progress about the fate of the local cinema. I think somebody wants to turn that into a supermarket too. I don't understand why, because we have millions already and nobody has any trouble finding things to buy – except for really useful things like metal mop buckets and shirt buttons and shoe laces, and you can bet they won't have those in the new supermarkets. Councils seems to be incapable of leaving well-enough alone. Some of the old York stone paving was broken, but that was because lorries had driven over it, and I see no reason to suppose that they won't break the pretty new stones too. What I wish *all* the councils would do is something about the sewers. I believe that all over the country the sewers are crumbling and one day the ground will open and swallow us up. This is a much worse prospect than breaking an ankle on a cracked pavement. The irony is that I banged my shin on a rod sticking out of a stone-cutting machine when I was trying to manoeuvre my way along Arlington Road to the supermarkets in between red and white cones and sand pits and signs and roped-off areas and workmen. I never fell over anything in the street before.

The other worry is what is going to happen to the neurotically compulsive among us. The sons have an acquaintance who once took about five hours getting round Holland Park because he wouldn't walk on the joins between the paving stones. What on earth he would do when faced with the prospect of the small stones and the very small ones I can't imagine. I suppose he would have to walk along the middle of the road where the articulated lorries would get him (if they weren't on the pavement again breaking the little stones). On the other hand if we're all going to fall into the sewers I suppose it doesn't matter. I just wish it could happen before Christmas.

Shop-worn

I heard a lady on the wireless the other day talking about shopping. She said it gave her an almost sexual thrill, that as she approached a bargain she felt positively orgasmic and started to salivate. Lucky old her was all I could say. I don't think she was talking about buying the bread and the sprouts and the fish fingers; she was on about buying clothes, but I don't believe I could work up a smidgeon of such enthusiasm if I'd gone out with the fixed intention of buying a diamond necklace and found one for 30 bob. I probably wouldn't buy it. I loathe shopping and have almost total sales resistance. I hate shops and shop assistants and bright lights and racks of frocks and piped music and handing over hard-earned cash; and poor Janet hates taking me shopping. After about five minutes I start whining about wanting to go home and insisting we don't have to buy shirts and underpants now. She can come back and do it by herself tomorrow. Shops are hot, unhealthy, airless places, and round Christmas time one always has one's coat on because it's cold in the streets. Head and feet ache and the discomfort is indescribable. Shops are always full too – full of garments (you never see any empty racks) and crammed with people – many with a sort of obsessive look in their eye and armsful of purchases.

Last week I saw a woman clutching half a dozen skirts and aiming for the cash desk. Had she lost all her other ones in a fire, or had she got five sisters? It's not the sort of question you can ask, but the speculation does something to ease the boredom. Another mystery is posed by the quantities of clothes that no one in her right mind would dream of buying – woollen skirts with lace inserts at the bottom, a shirtwaister in puce taffeta with a pussycat bow at the neck, multi-striped jumpers with sequinned butterflies, fringed thigh-length boots with base-metal buckles, although we did agree that the puce taffeta might just possibly not look out of place at a Conservative cocktail party. I've never been to one but I can sort of imagine it.

We were in Oxford Street yesterday and that was an odd experience in itself. There were traffic cops or meter maids or whatever they were, bellowing instructions through megaphones about when Christmas shoppers could and couldn't cross the road. This is new, isn't it? Or have I simply never noticed them before? Janet had a more entertaining time last week when a mad lady completely disregarded these instructions and sauntered back and forth in the teeth of the traffic shouting 'Hallelujah' and waving her arms, announcing she was saved. I think she'd probably overdosed on shopping and had decided never to do any any more. I have myself come close to insanity in Harrods and barely refrained from pushing over those tables laden with displays of unlikely-looking china. We once tried to buy a Hoover in Harrods and we couldn't find anyone willing to sell it to us. That's another aspect of shops. If you're 'just looking' you're mobbed by shop assistants, and if you sincerely wish to make a purchase hell could freeze over before one puts in an appearance. We found people prepared to sell us grand pianos and books and sofa-beds, but no one who was qualified to sell us a Hoover. We thought of grabbing one and going vroom vroom, and pushing it out of the place, pretending we were the cleaners; but in that case shop assistants would undoubtedly have appeared and our explanations have been disregarded.

I don't mind little shops so much. We went in one where the ratio of shop assistants to customers was the same; that is, there was me and Janet and two nice girls and, I have to admit, a lot of very decent clothes. The snag is, of course, that decent clothes in little shops tends to cost the earth, but by that time I was past caring. I had to have something to wear for Christmas or face the festivities in my petticoat, so I tried on a black velvet number. It looked a bit silly over socks and brogues, but we imagined patent-leather pumps, and one of the girls flung her pearls round my neck to show the effect, and we made an instant decision. You can't beat black velvet and pearls for looking lady-like, so I'll probably wear that to the end of my days and never have to go shopping again.

Jeremy Lewis

Playing for Time

Pitching and rolling on his first crossing of the Irish Sea, Jeremy Lewis fell instantly in love with a handsome, strong-featured girl in a corduroy coat, with auburn hair and an exciting-looking bosom – and remained so for the next eighteen months.

Having singularly failed to impress either himself or his employers in the world of advertising, he was now bound for Trinity College, Dublin, to embark upon an education that had little to do with the history course for which he had enrolled. Lured by the garrulous, genial charms of Dublin pubs, the inimitable characters with which the city overflows, the wild and beautiful countryside – it is little wonder academic aspirations began to wither away.

With a sharp eye for the absurd and a fond sympathy for life's eccentrics Jeremy Lewis treats us to uproarious tales from his time in Dublin in the sixties, tells of wild Irish islands, mad escapades in Europe and America, life amidst the snares and delusions involved in growing up in middle-class England in the 1950s, and of his ever unrequited passion for the ever unattainable ffenella . . .

'A minor masterpiece . . . anyone who reads *Playing for Time* without smiling should send for the undertaker'   *Irish Independent*

'A fizzily facetious saga of youth's mishaps'
                                                            John Carey, Sunday Times

'An unputdownable memoir . . . already I long for volume two'
                                                            A. N. Wilson

Flamingo

Alice Thomas Ellis

Home Life

Rarely, if ever, has the minefield of domestic life been charted as accurately as in Alice Thomas Ellis's *Spectator* column, 'Home Life'. With inimitable wit and perspicacity, she discourses on the vagaries of cats and neighbours, the recalcitrance of washing machines, the problems in getting to Wales and the even greater problems that inevitably await her there – reflections which strike a rueful chord with any harassed home-owner.

'Home Life' has won Alice Thomas Ellis an audience as wide as that for her much-praised novels, and here, in more permanent form, is a year's supply of these addictive articles.

'The funniest anthology I have read in years'   *The Times*

'One of those jewel-like volumes that might have come out of the eighteenth century, to be reprinted today as a classic of precise English, wit and womanly sensibility'
Valerie Grove, *London Standard*

Flamingo

Flamingo

Flamingo is a quality imprint publishing both fiction and non-fiction. Below are some recent titles.

Fiction
- ☐ CHANGES OF ADDRESS Lee Langley £3.95
- ☐ SHILOH & OTHER STORIES Bobbie Ann Mason £3.95
- ☐ BLACKPOOL VANISHES Richard Francis £3.95
- ☐ DREAMS OF SLEEP Josephine Humphreys £3.95
- ☐ THE ACCOMPANIST Nina Berberova £2.95
- ☐ SAD MOVIES Mark Linquist £3.95
- ☐ LITTLE RED ROOSTER Greg Matthews £3.95
- ☐ A PIECE OF MY HEART Richard Ford £3.95
- ☐ HER STORY Dan Jacobson £3.95
- ☐ WAR & PEACE IN MILTON KEYNES James Rogers £3.50
- ☐ PLATO PARK Carol Rumens £3.95
- ☐ GOING AFTER CACCIATO Tim O'Brien £3.95

Non-fiction
- ☐ CHINESE CHARACTERS Sarah Lloyd £3.95
- ☐ PLAYING FOR TIME Jeremy Lewis £3.95
- ☐ BEFORE THE OIL RAN OUT Ian Jack £3.95
- ☐ NATIVE STONES David Craig £3.95
- ☐ A WINTER'S TALE Fraser Harrison £3.50

You can buy Flamingo paperbacks at your local bookshop or newsagent. Or you can order them from Fontana Paperbacks, Cash Sales Department, Box 29, Douglas, Isle of Man. Please send a cheque, postal or money order (not currency) worth the purchase price plus 22p per book (or plus 22p per book if outside the UK).

NAME (Block letters) _____

ADDRESS_____

_____

_____